REFLECTIONS ON GENDER AND SCIENCE

Reflections on Gender and Science

Evelyn Fox Keller

YALE UNIVERSITY PRESS
New Haven and London

Designed by Margaret E. B. Joyner
and set in Caledonia and Optima Medium type.
Printed in the United States of America by
Vail-Ballou, Binghamton, N.Y.

Library of Congress Cataloging in Publication Data

Keller, Evelyn Fox, 1936–
    Reflections on gender and science.

    Bibliography: p.
    Includes index.
    1. Science—Philosophy.   2. Women in science.
3. Science—History.   I. Title.
Q175.K28   1985   501   84-17327
ISBN 0–300–03291–9 (alk. paper)
        0–300–03636–1 (pbk.)
The paper in this book meets the guidelines for permanence
and durability of the Committee on Production Guidelines
for Book Longevity of the Council on Library Resources.
13   12   11   10   9   8   7   6   5   4   3

Contents

Acknowledgments

Adequate acknowledgment of all of the many friends and colleagues who contributed to the development of the ideas of this work would require a more comprehensive and more conscious view of my own development than I can claim. This book began almost a decade ago when, inspired by other work in feminist studies, I first conceived of gender and science as a subject for inquiry. During the intervening years, as I struggled to find meaningful ways to pose the questions that constitute this subject, I sought assistance from everyone I knew and from everything I read. My principal debt is thus to a community extending beyond immediate friends and colleagues to include all those who contributed to the collective endeavor of feminist theory that was emerging over this period.

More specifically, virtually every friend who was willing was recruited to read early drafts of the first articles I wrote. Bell Chevigny, Christine Grontkowski, Lebert Harris, Helene Moglen, Sara Ruddick, and Seth Schein were but a few of those who provided invaluable support and patient criticism in the days before any public response to my work was available. As I began to lecture on this subject and to publish in the professional journals, the responses of many others helped to clarify and sharpen my own thinking. Somewhere around this time, Thomas S. Kuhn became a friend, and he too was recruited. My debt to Kuhn for his careful readings and incisive criticism of drafts of all the material in this book is immeasurable.

Over the last two years, others provided additional support in the writing, organizing, and polishing of the final manuscript. I am grateful to Carolyn Cohen, N. Katherine Hayles, Hilde Hein, Martin Krieger, Ruth Perry, Sharon Traweek, Marilyn Young, and others for their critical readings of various chapters. The support of Myra

Jehlen is perhaps most directly responsible for the actual completion of this manuscript. Her daily encouragement and intelligent counsel throughout the summer of 1983 helped me over the most difficult hurdle of all—the task of putting a final manuscript in order.

Once completed, the entire manuscript was read—in some cases, heroically reread—by Susan Contratto, Thomas S. Kuhn, Helene Moglen, William and Sara Ruddick, and Silvan S. Schweber. Their encouragement gave me the extra energy I needed for the final revisions, and their suggestions provided the basis for these revisions. But my largest debt in this stage of the work is to the sensitivity and unstinting support of my editor, Jehane Burns Kuhn. Above all, her unfailing eye for meaning has helped me, as it did once before, to articulate and even think my own thoughts more clearly.

Gladys Topkis at Yale University Press contributed advocacy and enthusiasm—as well as editorial suggestions—of the kind that authors always hope for. Carl Kaysen generously extended the hospitality of the Program in Science, Technology and Society at MIT, and Dean Richard Astro and other colleagues at Northeastern University helped to provide me with a working environment that made it possible to complete this book.

My teachers have been many, but none has taught me more than my children. My daughter's courage and fortitude in her own adolescent struggles have been an inspiration to me, and my son's unfailing support of a project so different from his own endeavors has served as a model of loving generosity. It is to them that I dedicate this book.

REFLECTIONS ON GENDER AND SCIENCE

Introduction

Representation of the world, like the world itself, is
the work of men; they describe it from their own point
of view, which they confuse with the absolute truth.

SIMONE DE BEAUVOIR (1970)

A decade ago, I was deeply engaged (if not quite fully content) in
my work as a mathematical biophysicist. I believed wholeheartedly
in the laws of physics, and in their place at the apex of knowledge.
Sometime in the mid-1970s—overnight, as it were—another kind
of question took precedence, upsetting my entire intellectual hierarchy: How much of the nature of science is bound up with the idea
of masculinity, and what would it mean for science if it were otherwise? A lifelong training had labeled that question patently absurd;
but once I actually heard it, I could not, either as a woman or as a
scientist, any longer avoid it. Gradually, I began to explore the relation between gender and science in a series of essays; nine of these
are collected here.

More recently, a former professor of mine, having heard of my
work on gender and science, asked me to tell him just what it was
that I have learned about women. I tried to explain, "It's not women
I am learning about so much as men. Even more, it is science." The
difference is important, and the misunderstanding (not his alone),
revealing.

The widespread assumption that a study of gender and science
could only be a study of women still amazes me: if women are made
rather than born, then surely the same is true of men. It is also true
of science. The essays in this book are premised on the recognition
that both gender and science are socially constructed categories.

3

Science is the name we give to a set of practices and a body of
knowledge delineated by a community, not simply defined by the
exigencies of logical proof and experimental verification. Similarly,
masculine and feminine are categories defined by a culture, not by
biological necessity. Women, men, and science are created, together, out of a complex dynamic of interwoven cognitive, emotional,
and social forces. The focus of these essays is on that dynamic and
the ways it supports both the historic conjunction of science and
masculinity, and the equally historic disjunction between science
and femininity. My subject, therefore, is not women per se, or even
women and science: it is the making of men, women, and science,
or, more precisely, how the making of men and women has affected
the making of science.

Such a venture comes into being with the meeting of two apparently independent developments in recent scholarship: feminist
theory and the social studies of science. The second has changed
our thinking about the relation between science and society—without, however, considering the role of gender—and the first has
changed our thinking about the relation between gender and society
but has been only peripherally concerned with science. As productive as each of these developments has been in its own terms, each
leaves critical gaps in our understanding that the other can help to
fill. Furthermore, their conjunction enables us to identify the critical
role of gender ideology in mediating between science and social
forms. I begin, therefore, with a brief review of these developments—of the progress that has been made and the problems that
remain.

The social studies of science address the task of locating the development of science in its social and political context. A recent critical
impetus for this endeavor came more than two decades ago, with
the publication of T. S. Kuhn's *The Structure of Scientific Revolutions* (1962). A major contribution of Kuhn was to demonstrate,
by examining specific examples in the history of science, that scientific revolutions cannot be explained by the arrival of a better
theory according to any simple scientific criteria. "Ordinarily," he
writes, "it is only much later, after the new paradigm has been
developed, accepted, and exploited, that apparently decisive argu-

ments are made" (p. 156). In the view that Kuhn puts forth, science remains progressive in the sense that the investment of scientific energy is productive: it produces, over time, theories with wider explanatory power than could have existed without that investment. But the change in direction that new theories dictate, the change in world view that they lead to, is not in itself simply determined by internal logic. Other factors—above and beyond empirical evidence and theoretical necessity—enter into the community's choice of a "best theory."

The direct implication of such a claim is that not only different collections of facts, different focal points of scientific attention, but also different organizations of knowledge, different interpretations of the world, are both possible and consistent with what we call science.

Kuhn's work, paralleling the conclusions of a number of other historians of science, came at a propitious time. It provided a welcome alternative to the view maintained by scientists themselves, and until then unchallenged by most historians: the view that science is autonomous and absolutely progressive—approximating ever more closely a full and accurate description of reality "as it is."

Although Kuhn himself did not undertake to map out the influence of other, extrascientific factors affecting choice of scientific theories, others did. In the intervening years a growing number of historians and sociologists of science, reading Kuhan's work as support for the proposition that scientific neutrality reflects ideology more than actual history, have sought to identify the political and social forces affecting the growth of scientific knowledge.

The body of literature that has emerged from this effort has irrevocably changed the way many people—especially nonscientists—think about science. Kuhn's argument, originally so provocative, has come to seem commonplace—even, to many, too cautious. The proposition that science is subject to the influence of special interests has been transformed, in some quarters, to relativism—to the view that science is nothing but the expression of special interests. Yet, while our sensitivity to the influence of social and political forces has certainly grown, our understanding of their actual impact on the production of scientific theory has not.

Partly as a result of this failure, the impact of the social studies of science on the way most scientists think about their own work has been only marginal. Working scientists may agree that political pressures affect the uses, and even the focus, of scientific research; but they fail to see how such pressures can affect their results, the description of nature that emerges from their desks and laboratories. For the most part, they continue to share the view expressed by Stephen Weinberg (1974, p. 43): "The laws of nature are as impersonal and free of human values as the rules of arithmetic. We didn't want it to come out that way, but it did."

The net result is that discourse about science continues for the most part on two noncommunicating levels: one an increasingly radical critique that fails to account for the effectiveness of science, and the other a justification that draws confidence from that effectiveness to maintain a traditional, and essentially unchanged, philosophy of science. What is needed is a way of thinking and talking about science that can make sense of these two very different perspectives—that can credit the realities they each reflect and yet account for their differences in perception.

The political ferment of the 1960s that helped to fuel recent developments in the social studies of science also gave impetus to the women's movement, and, in turn, to the development of feminist theory. A principal task of feminist theory has been to redress the absence of women in the history of social and political thought. Above all, this effort has given rise to a form of attention, a lens that brings into focus a particular question: What does it mean to call one aspect of human experience male and another female? How do such labels affect the ways in which we structure our experiential world, assign value to its different domains, and, in turn, acculturate and value actual men and women? Over the last decade, such questions have led to a radical critique of traditional scholarly disciplines, requiring a major reexamination of many of the fundamental assumptions prevailing in psychology, economics, history, literature— all the fields of the humanities and social sciences. In the last few years, encouraged by recent developments in the history and sociology of science, feminist scholars have begun to turn their attention to the natural (or "hard") sciences.

The most immediate issue for a feminist perspective on the natural sciences is the deeply rooted popular mythology that casts objectivity, reason, and mind as male, and subjectivity, feeling, and nature as female. In this division of emotional and intellectual labor, women have been the guarantors and protectors of the personal, the emotional, the particular, whereas science—the province par excellence of the impersonal, the rational, and the general—has been the preserve of men.

The consequence of such a division is not simply the exclusion of women from the practice of science. That exclusion itself is a symptom of a wider and deeper rift between feminine and masculine, subjective and objective, indeed between love and power—a rending of the human fabric that affects all of us, as women and men, as members of a society, and even as scientists.

The same division also effects the very terms in which science has been criticized. One can argue that it is precisely this division that is responsible for two notable omissions in most social studies of science. First is the failure to take serious notice not only of the fact that science has been produced by a particular subset of the human race—that is, almost entirely by white, middle-class men— but also of the fact that it has evolved under the formative influence of a particular ideal of masculinity. For the founding fathers of modern science, the reliance on the language of gender was explicit: They sought a philosophy that deserved to be called "masculine," that could be distinguished from its ineffective predecessors by its "virile" power, its capacity to bind Nature to man's service and make her his slave (Bacon).

Second, and related, is the fact that, in its attempts to identify extrascientific determinants of the growth of scientific knowledge, the social studies of science have for the most part ignored the influence of those forces (disregarded as idiosyncratic and at the same time transsocial), that are at work in the individual human psyche. Just as science is not the purely cognitive endeavor we once thought it, neither is it as impersonal as we thought: science is a deeply personal as well as a social activity.

In other words, despite its rejection of "scientific neutrality," the social study of science has pursued its critique in terms that tacitly support the divisions between public and private, impersonal and personal, and masculine and feminine: divisions that continue to secure the autonomy of science. A feminist perspective leads us to proceed quite differently. It leads us to identify these divisions as central to the basic structure of modern science and society. We see our world divided by a multiplicity of conceptual and social dichotomies—mutually sanctioning, mutually supportive, and mutually defining: public *or* private, masculine *or* feminine, objective *or* subjective, power *or* love. Thus, for example, the division between objective fact and subjective feeling is sustained by the association of objectivity with power and masculinity, and its remove from the world of women and love. In turn, the disjunction of male from female is sustained by the association of masculinity with power and objectivity, and its disjunction from subjectivity and love. And so on.

A feminist perspective on science confronts us with the task of examining the roots, dynamics, and consequences of this interacting network of associations and disjunctions—together constituting what might be called the "science-gender system." It leads us to ask how ideologies of gender and science inform each other in their mutual construction, how that construction functions in our social arrangements, and how it affects men and women, science and nature. But feminism not only provides us with a subject; it also provides us with a particular method of analysis for investigating that subject. Because that method so deeply informs my own procedures, I need to say a little more about the logic of feminist analysis.

A decade ago, "the personal is political" was an aphorism—perhaps the clearest expression of what is distinctive about the modern feminist movement. Today, feminist thinkers recognize the conjunction of personal and political as more than an aphorism: they see it as a method. As Catherine McKinnon has written,

> the personal as political is not a simile, not a metaphor, and not an analogy. . . . It means that women's distinctive experience as women occurs within that sphere that has been socially lived as the personal—private, emotional, interiorized, particular, individuated, intimate—so that what it is to know the politics of woman's situation is to know women's personal lives. (1982, p. 534)

The converse of this would seem to be that to know the politics of man's situation is to know men's apersonal lives. But men's lives are apersonal *because* and to the extent that women's lives are personal. The apersonal politics of public man still depends critically on his marriage to domesticized, private woman; his rationality is premised on her capacity to embody the emotion of which reason has been cleansed. In other words, the political reveals its personal content by its dependence on a programmatic division between public and private, a division that is itself a political construction with personal meaning. The demarcation between public and private not only defines and defends the boundaries of the political but also helps form its content and style. Feminist analysis began by rejecting that demarcation, showing how the private bears on the public, as well as the public on the personal; it revealed the personal as political and the political as personal.

The work of many feminist scholars now gives us the courage to carry the logic of this analysis one stage further: The same demarcation, even more fiercely defended, provokes us to explore the interdependencies between subjectivity and objectivity, between feeling and reason. In short, the logical extension of the personal as political is the scientific as personal.

This logic, pursued systematically, adds to our critical thinking about science the kind of thinking that is often said to be "just like a woman," while at the same time undercutting the division of labor on which such a judgment is based. Feminism makes a unique contribution to more traditional studies of science; it encourages the use of expertise that has traditionally belonged to women—not simply as a woman's perspective but as a critical instrument for examining the roots of those dichotomies that isolate this perspective and deny its legitimacy. It seeks to enlarge our understanding of the history, philosophy, and sociology of science through the inclusion not only of women and their actual experiences but also of those domains of human experience that have been relegated to women: namely, the personal, the emotional, and the sexual.

Of course, to focus on the personal, emotional, and sexual dimensions of the construction and acceptance of claims to scientific knowledge is, precisely because of the male-centeredness of this tradition, to focus on the personal, emotional, and sexual dimensions of male experience. In one sense, it is to pursue in earnest the commonplace wisdom so eloquently expressed by Mary Ellman. Faced with the charge that "women always get personal," Ellman counters: "I'd say, men always get impersonal. If you hurt their feelings, they make Boyle's law out of it!" (1968, p. xiii).

Such an inversion of the personal and impersonal constitutes a far more radical, and correspondingly more problematic, challenge to traditional conceptions of objectivity than that initiated by recent historians and sociologists of science. It suggests that our "laws of nature" are more than simple expressions of the results of objective inquiry or of political and social pressures: they must also be read for their personal—and by tradition, masculine—content. It uncovers, in short, the personal investment scientists make in impersonality; the anonymity of the picture they produce is revealed as itself a kind of signature.

At the same time, however, this inversion also suggests a way of bridging the gulf between the claims made within the scientific community and those of its outside critics—that is, between "internalist" and "externalist" discourse on science. Attention to the intrapersonal dynamics of "theory choice" illuminates some of the subtler means by which ideology manifests itself in science—even in the face of scientists' best intentions. It permits us to make sense of (without necessarily sharing) the enduring faith that most working scientists have, even under current critical siege, in the objectivity of their enterprise. In particular, the psychological coherence of the impulse toward impersonality suggests a continuity between ideology, personal motivation, and impersonal product. This continuity accounts, first, for the attraction of certain individuals to the image that science projects and, second, for the (largely unwitting) attraction of those individuals to particular interpretations of both science and nature. It suggests, for example, that scientists who are "driven to escape from personal existence to the world of objective observing and understanding" (Einstein, quoted in Holton 1974, p. 69) actively embrace—even choose—a picture of reality as being "as impersonal and free of human values as the rules of arithmetic"; that scientists, as human actors, find some pictures or theories more persuasive and even more self-evident than others in part because of the conformation of those pictures or theories to their prior emotional commitments, expectations, and desires.

The fact that Boyle's law is not wrong must, however, not be forgotten. Any effective critique of science needs to take due account of the undeniable successes of science as well as of the commitments that have made such successes possible. If individuals tend to be drawn to science by the desire (or need) to escape the personal, or by the promise of quasi-religious communion, they are also drawn by another, equally personal but perhaps more universal, ambition: namely, the search for reliable, shareable knowledge of the world around us. Indeed, scientists' shared commitment to the possibility of reliable knowledge of nature, and to its dependence on experimental replicability and logical coherence, is an indispensable prerequisite for the effectiveness of any scientific venture. What needs to be understood is how these conscious commitments (commitments we can all share) are fueled and elaborated, and sometimes also subverted, by the more parochial social, political, and emotional commitments (conscious or not) of particular individuals and groups.

Boyle's law does give us a reliable description of the relation between pressure and volume in low density gases at high temperatures, a description that stands the tests of experimental replicability and logical coherence. But it is crucial to recognize that it is a statement about a particular set of phenomena, prescribed to meet particular interests and described in accordance with certain agreed-upon criteria of both reliability and utility. Judgments about which phenomena are worth studying, which kinds of data are significant—as well as which descriptions (or theories) of those phenomena are most adequate, satisfying, useful, and even reliable—depend critically on the social, linguistic, and scientific practices of those making the judgments in question. This dependency is more fully elaborated in the introduction to part 3 of this book (as well as in the essays of that section); for now, my point is merely that the success of Boyle's law must be recognized as circumscribed and hence limited by the context in which it arises.

Predilections based on emotional (as well as social and political) commitments express themselves precisely in the domain of those social and linguistic practices that help determine, within the scientific community, the priority of interests and the criteria of success. It is through these day-to-day practices that the selection of preferred descriptions and the dismissal of less congenial ones take place; this is where the truly subversive force of ideology makes itself felt.

An objectivist ideology, prematurely proclaiming anonymity, disinterest, and impersonality and radically excluding the subject, imposes a veil over these practices, a veil not so much of secrecy as of tautology. Apparent self-evidence renders them invisible and hence inaccessible to criticism. The effort toward universality closes in on itself, and parochiality is protected. In this way the ideology of scientific objectivity belies its own aims, subverting both the meaning and the potential of objective inquiry.

If the pursuit of scientific knowledge is to be reclaimed as a universal goal, certain characteristics of that pursuit need to be recognized as constant and indispensable. But others, taken on by communities of scientists as they have evolved, are more parochial—habits acquired unselfconsciously and, equally unselfconsciously, internalized and taken for granted. Thus, scientists in every discipline live and work with assumptions that feel like constants ("that's what good science is") but that are in fact variable, and, given the right kind of jolt, subject to change. Such parochialities, like any other communal practice, can be perceived only through the lens of difference, by stepping outside the community.

As a woman and a scientist, the status of outsider came to me gratis. Feminism enabled me to exploit that status as a privilege. I began to see the network of gender associations in the characteristic language of science as neither natural nor self-evident, but as contingent, and dismaying. I began to see further that these were not just ornamental images on the surface of scientific rhetoric; they were deeply embedded in the structure of scientific ideology, with recognizable implications for practice. Each of the essays in this book examines and questions that network of associations: in the first section, historically; in the second section, psychoanalytically; and in the third section, scientifically and philosophically. Clearly, these inquiries presuppose a judgment, a desire on my part for change—both in the practice of science and in the place of science in our culture. My interest in change, in alternative scenarios and shifts in language, is evident throughout, but the kinds of changes I look for in science—natural consequences of the changes in language I advocate—are most explicitly indicated in the essays of the third section. Together, the essays in all three sections outline and begin to chart a terrain that amounts to a psychosociology of scientific knowledge.

Each essay is more or less self-contained, written with a particular focus, addressing these questions from a particular perspective. The variation among them has been helpful to me; it may also be useful to the reader. I suggest that, given the complexity of this new terrain, the variety of perspectives may even be necessary to its definition. Several of the essays have been previously published and reprinted here with little revision. It seems to me that an attempt to rewrite them to represent a unified perspective would subvert part of their purpose.

The three sections—historical, psychological, and scientific/philosophical—are ordered as they are to allow for maximum recursiveness. Themes presented in each essay are often indirectly, if not directly, drawn upon in the essays that follow. Each section is prefaced by an introduction of its own.

PART ONE

Historical Couplings of Mind and Nature

Nature is to man whatever name he wants to give her. He will perceive nature according to the names he gives her, according to the relation and perspective he chooses.

ERNEST SCHACHTEL (1959, p. 202)

Naming nature is the special business of science. Theories, models, and descriptions are elaborated names. In these acts of naming, the scientist simultaneously constructs and contains nature—"according to the relation and perspective he chooses." The individual scientist of course does not choose his or her "relation and perspective" freely; they are part of the process of socialization into the scientific community and into the culture of which that community is a part. Relation and perspective thus constitute the first stage of naming: the stage that frames the linguistic subset available to the working scientist.

But if naming nature is the special business of science, naming science is the responsibility of society. People everywhere have sought some form of reliable knowledge of the natural world. But if we define science in the way the term is usually used—by what it is that those individuals we now call scientists do—then we are speaking of a particular form this pursuit has taken in Western society, a form that has been developing since the seventeenth century. Although the precise delineation of this form is made difficult by the variety of practices subsumed under the rubric *science*, its normative dimensions—the values, goals, and assumptions that comprise the ideology of modern science—are relatively clear. In order

17

to understand how these norms affect the pursuit of scientific knowledge, it is useful to step back and inquire about alternate forms that similar ambitions have taken in the past. When we do, we discover not only that our conception of how to seek reliable knowledge of the natural world has varied over time and place, but also that our definitions of knowledge and of nature have .varied with them.

Beneath these variations, the primary question for all visions of science is how we can know. This question takes two forms: first theoretical—what makes knowledge possible—and second practical—how we are able to achieve that knowledge. Inevitably, the answers to both are linked by the underlying images of mind and nature, subject and object. These underlying images dictate the relation between mind and nature that must be assumed in order to account for knowledge; once assumed, that relation inevitably guides inquiry. Without mediation, commonality, or intercourse between subject and object, knowledge is not possible.

One of the most common metaphors in Western history for such mediation has been the sexual relation: knowledge is a form of consummation, just as sex is a form of knowledge. Both are propelled by desire. Whether in fantasy, experience, or linguistic trope, sexual union remains the most compelling and most primal instance of the act of knowing. Even when unrecognized by metaphor, the experience of knowing is rooted in the carnal. It does not, however, remain there. What classically distinguishes knowledge is its essential thrust away from the body: its ambition is to transcend the carnal. Mind is not simply immanent in matter; it is transcendent over it. All visions of knowledge must accordingly struggle with the dialectic between immanence and transcendence. What is especially striking is how often the metaphoric field for this struggle is that of sex and gender, and, I shall argue, how deeply those metaphors have influenced the disciplines of knowledge.

But if the centrality of sex to conceptions of knowledge is invariant in Western cultural traditions, the meaning of sex and gender is not. In each culture, conceptions of sex and gender reflect the longings and fears of the individuals who gave them voice, as well as the overall character of the societies that embraced them as their own. To illustrate how differences in conceptions of sex and gender bear upon conceptions of knowledge, I have chosen three moments in Western intellectual history, exhibiting three alternative relations to and perspectives of nature that have been present in the prehistory and early history of science. Each is illustrative of a different science-gender system. All three moments, closely intertwined, are still present in our modern heritage, but the disparities among them are a key to a recognition of what is culturally specific to the particular relation of mind to nature on which our own science is based.

The first essay in this section, chapter 1, examines the sexual imagery of Plato's dialogues. This imagery, informed as it is by the sexual mores of Athenian culture, provides a crucial substructure to Plato's philosophical work; its analysis reveals a parsing of sexuality into eros and aggression in Platonic epistemology that has continued to reverberate throughout Western intellectual history. Plato's own use of this separation was, however, distinctive. By restricting knowledge to the domain of theory (as distinct from experiment), and nature to the realm of forms (as distinct from matter), Plato is able to map out a path to knowledge guided by love, and insulated from the aggression both he and his culture associate with sensible, material, and female nature.

More than two thousand years later, Francis Bacon offers another description of a path to knowledge. But Bacon's ideal of knowledge is experimental rather than theoretical; the object of knowledge he has in mind is the concrete, material world—not the world of abstract forms. For Bacon, as for Plato, the principal metaphor is sexual. But Bacon's metaphor, unlike Plato's, is a primarily heterosexual rather than homoerotic relation: a heterosexual relation in fact not very different from the stereotypic marriage of Plato's time. Accordingly, Bacon's marital imagery carries with it much of the aggression that Plato had managed to avoid. Even so, a crucial ambiguity remains in Bacon's writings: his imagery is not purely heterosexual or wholly masculine. Chapter 2, "Baconian Science: The Arts of Mastery and Obedience," explores these ambiguities through an analysis of Bacon's own language. The original version of this essay was published in 1980.

Chapter 3 examines the language of sex and gender in some of the debates that surrounded the "birth" of modern science. It focuses in particular on the contest, in the decades immediately preceding the founding of the Royal Society, between two different visions of a "new science," roughly described as the mechanical and the hermetical philosophies. I argue that the "mechanical" philosophical commitments that came to prevail both reflected and helped solidify a polarization of masculine and feminine that was central to the formation of early industrial capitalist society. Ultimately, the principal point of this essay is to suggest that gender ideology can be seen as a critical mediator among the social, political, and intellectual origins of modern science.

CHAPTER ONE

Love and Sex in Plato's Epistemology

> You need not know of the doctrines and writings of
> the great masters of antiquity, of Plato and Aristotle,
> you need never have heard their names, none the less
> you are under the spell of their authority. . . . Our
> entire thinking, the logical categories in which it
> moves, the linguistic patterns it uses (being therefore
> dominated by them)—all this . . . is, in the main, the
> product of the great thinkers of antiquity.
>
> GOMPERZ, quoted in Schrödinger (1954)

Plato was the first writer in Western intellectual history to make
explicit and systematic use of the language of sexuality for knowing.
Indeed, his use of sexual language—becoming more explicit in direct proportion to the proximity of the knower to the known— suggests a philosophical function for his sexual metaphors that requires
explication in and of itself. To that end, it is useful to begin by
locating Plato's philosophical efforts in historical context and relating
them to the problematic he inherited from his culture.

For Plato, as for earlier Greek thinkers, mind and nature were
bound by a common essence and divided by an essential difference.
Their commonality was granted by what amounts to linguistic guarantee. The use of the word *logos* (referring at once to a property of
mind and to a property of the world) both reflects and sanctions the
conceptual linkage between the two. Its double meaning survives
in the ambiguity of the word *rational. Logos* refers simultaneously
to that which is accountable, or measurable, and to that mode of

21

thought which generates accounts, or reasons. Early Greek thinkers "had endowed physical nature itself with the attributes of reason. . . . They had been so absorbed in the discovery that nature was rational that they never stopped to distinguish between the categories of intelligibility and intelligence. . . . Logos 'accounts,' both in the active sense of accounting and in the objective sense of the character of things which makes them capable of being so accounted" (Vlastos 1970, p. 89) This property of rationality, a property shared by both mind and nature, constituted a symmetrical bond between the two. Mind was natural, and nature was suffused with mind. "Greek natural science was based on the principle that the world of nature is saturated or permeated by mind. Greek thinkers regarded the presence of mind in nature as the source of that regularity or orderliness in the natural world whose presence made a science of nature possible" (Collingwood, 1945, p. 3).

Nature, however, is not completely bound by Logos: it remains caught in an essential duality. If in some respects it is subject to the light of reason and order, it is also enmired in the dark forces of unreason and disorder. The forces of unreason, in Greek mythology and drama most often embodied in the earth goddesses or the Furies, are never fully vanquished, even when they are subdued. Mind, itself never fully extricated from the body, can and must struggle to free the soul from the clutches of passion and the flesh; reason, as in Aeschylus's *Oresteia*, may even succeed in persuading unreason. But deep in the bowels of the earth, the Furies retain their power.

Plato's self-imposed task is to forge a theory of knowledge that is immune to the subversive powers of the irrational, that allows mind to achieve transcendence even while it remains compromised by immanence. His solution is radical: It is to define the proper object of knowledge as lying entirely outside the domain of temporal, material nature. Mind undergoes a parallel purification: As nature is dematerialized, so is mind disembodied. For Plato, truth is accessible only in the realm of pure and absolute being, a realm reached not by directing mind's gaze away from matter but by learning to see through and beyond the realm of the merely physical. Only then can a true meeting, or conjunction, of mind and nature occur. Knowledge is a form of recognition imaged on vision. Just as the eye recognizes an object through the intermingling of rays of light emanating from both, so the recognition of form by mind is achieved by a union of two kindred essences.[1] The philosopher strives to "grasp the essential nature of things with the mental faculty fitted to do so," that is, with "the faculty which is akin to reality, and which approaches and unites with it" (Republic, 490b).[2]

In Plato's epistemology, mutable matter has been left behind, abandoned to the forces of the "irrational, the fortuitous and the disorderly" (Vlastos 1970, p. 89). The question remains, however: How does mind, embedded in a mortal body, find its way toward truth? Plato's answer, spelled out in the Symposium, is striking: mind discovers knowledge when guided by Eros. "When a man, starting from this sensible world and making his way upward by a right use of his feeling of love . . . , begins to catch sight of that [eternal] beauty, he is very near his goal" (212a). Furthermore, when a man "sees beauty with the faculty capable of seeing it, [he will] be able to bring forth not mere images of goodness but true goodness" (212c). In short, as desire begets love, so does love beget knowledge.

But not all desire begets love, nor does all love beget knowledge. Eros pulls the soul in two directions, toward reason and toward passion, toward the sublime and toward the sordid. The dialectic between transcendence and immanence is now played out in the realm of Eros. And it is to this realm that Plato continually returns.

One way to characterize Plato's struggle would be as the struggle between unity and difference. The image of Eros brilliantly reflects the fundamental problem of knowledge: How can difference be resolved into unity, subject be wedded to object, becoming be transformed into being? Repeatedly, Plato attempts to simplify the struggle between difference and unity by a prior division, but over and over again his dilemma returns. Indeed, one might read the Platonic dialogues as successive attacks on the inadequacies of division as a guarantee of unity.[3] Two fundamental divisions persist

1. This argument is more fully developed in Keller and Grontkowski (1983).
2. "Unites" is translated from the Greek word *suneimi*, which is also used to denote sexual intercourse (Seth Schein, personal communication).
3. In the later dialogues (especially *Sophist*, *Statesman*, and the end of *Phaedrus*), division is explicitly the method par excellence for approaching the unity of knowledge.

through all his efforts. First, there is the distinction between logical and physical nature, and second, in close parallel, the distinction between homosexual and heterosexual Eros.

Heterosexual desire does not contribute to transcendence, for Plato, precisely because of its association with physical procreation. As Diotima explains in the *Symposium*, "Those whose creative instinct is physical have recourse to women, and show their love in this way, believing that by begetting children they can secure for themselves an immortal and blessed memory hereafter forever; but there are some whose creative desire is of the soul, and who long to beget spiritually, not physically, the progeny which it is the nature of the soul to create and bring to birth" (209b). Only desire of the soul—"desire for the perpetual possession of the good" (206a)— leads to procreation in the realm of Being. Diotima adds, "If you ask what that progeny is, it is wisdom and virtue in general" (209b). And despite the fact that it is a woman who here articulates the virtues of desire, Plato's model for spiritual begetting is the love of man for man; knowledge is a product of a divine union of kindred essences. It is a man's feeling of love for boys, not for women, that provides the first impetus for the philosopher's journey. The union of mind with "the essential nature of things" is a union of like with like; accordingly, it is taken for granted throughout the *Symposium* and the *Phaedrus* "that eros which is significant as a step towards the world of Being is homosexual" (Dover 1980, p. 162).

But just as mind remains embedded in matter, so even homosexual Eros continues to reside in bodies: the love of man for man remains inextricably compounded of bodily and spiritual desire, in ways that constantly threaten the division between transcendence and immanence. Indeed, the surrender to physical desire reduces homosexual Eros to the status of heterosexual, or animal, desire. A man overcome by physical desire is merely "eager like a four-footed beast to mate and to beget children, or in his addiction to wantonness feels no fear or shame in pursuing a pleasure which is unnatural" (*Phaedrus*, 250e). The soul is rent, even in a world already simplified by partitioning male from female: division again fails to suffice as a guarantor of unity.

In sex as in knowledge, the tension between unity and difference generates harmonics that grow more and more complex as they reverberate with the tension between love and aggression, equality and hierarchy, cooperation and domination. These are strains that can be heard throughout all the Platonic dialogues, but especially where Eros emerges explicitly as the guide to Truth, in the *Symposium* and *Phaedrus*. To see how the sexual model functions in Plato's epistemological strategies, however, one needs first to understand more about the sexual ethos and gender ideology of his time.

The first observation to be made is the familiar one that Plato's distinction between homosexual and heterosexual Eros echoes a division institutionalized in his larger culture. The extent to which Attic wives and husbands lived in separate spheres can be judged in part from the extent to which marriage was limited to the purposes of procreation. For objects of sexual desire, the Athenian male citizen typically looked elsewhere—to female courtesans or to other males. Yet, even within the range of male homosexual activity, a further division held sway in Greek convention, as in Plato's writings. Sexual coupling between social peers was sharply differentiated, both in mode of intercourse and in level of acceptability, from sex between citizen on the one hand and slave, foreigner, or prostitute on the other. As a consequence, not two but three models of sexual relations prevailed, corresponding to three radically different forms of relationship and degrees of respectability. (Sexual relations between women, in Athens at least, were for the most part simply ignored.)

The most highly valued by far, and the only model relevant to Plato, was a relationship between an adult male (the *erastes*, or lover) and a youth of comparable social standing (the *eromenos*, or beloved). This relationship was distinguished from both sodomy and heterosexual intercourse in several crucial respects. Although typically between an older and a younger man, it was the only sexual relation obtaining between social equals; it was also the only sexual relation normally consummated in face-to-face position, in intercrural intercourse. As Dover (1980) concludes from his examination of Attic vase paintings, "The intercrural mode is normal when the sexual object is male, but unknown when it is female" (p. 99). The most commonly portrayed position for heterosexual intercourse is from the rear, with "the woman bending over while the man stands and penetrates her from behind and below" (p. 100)—a position, in short, resembling homosexual anal copulation, also commonly depicted in the vase paintings, and almost universally indicating dominance. In terms of actual modes of intercourse, the relation between *erastes* and *eromenos* (the pederastic relation) is distinguished by its avoidance of the division between dominant and subordinate, characteristic of both heterosexual intercourse and homosexual anal copulation. The line between the two forms of homosexual intercourse is crucial. A man who assumes the submissive role violates the conventions of "legitimate Eros." He is seen as abandoning his integrity, acquiescing in an act of aggression against himself, and accordingly forfeiting his role as an Athenian citizen; he "detaches himself from the ranks of male citizenry and classifies himself with women and foreigners" (p. 103). Worse yet, "Any man believed to have done whatever his senior homosexual partner wanted him to do is assumed to have prostituted himself" (p. 103). In either case, he has abandoned his claim to masculinity.

Central to the legitimacy of the pederastic relation is thus the maintenance of dignity, particularly on the part of the one who is loved. Not only must the *eromenos* demonstrate a refusal to submit to the will of his *erastes*; of equal importance is the constraint that he not share in the older man's desire. In the vase paintings of classical Greece, only women and degraded men are depicted as experiencing positive sexual enjoyment in the passive role. By contrast, the *eromenos* stares dispassionately ahead. He may feel affection, but never sexual desire. As Xenophon remarks, "The boy does not share in the man's pleasure in intercourse, as a woman does; cold sober, he looks upon the other drunk with sexual desire" (Xenophon's *Symposium*, 8.21, quoted in Dover, p. 52). Men *may* feel desire without compromising their masculinity, but only by assuming the active role. It is thus not desire as such that assimilates men to women, but the conjunction of desire with passivity—a conjunction seen not only permitting but inviting aggressive domination.

"Legitimate Eros"—premised on both mutual consent and respect—is set apart from illegitimate homosexuality precisely by managing to avoid all such aggressive and submissive connotations. That it does so is not simply a consequence of the social equality of the participants but rather depends on a delicate balance between equality and hierarchy. The symmetry in social status is played off against the asymmetry in age, on the one hand, and against the distribution of sexual desire, on the other. To be a lover is to be older and wiser but, at the same time, to be the slave of desire. The beloved, "subordinate neither to sexual pleasure nor to [his] sexual partner" (Golden, 1981, p. 129), is able to redress the imbalance and preserve his dignity precisely because he is not overcome or enslaved by emotion. The dynamic is resolved toward equality, but it retains the imprint of its own internal hierarchies.

In sum, then, the pederastic relation could be said to have offered a model of unreciprocal but relatively equitable sexuality, in a culture that acknowledged no model of reciprocal sexuality between equals. Such a model fit Plato's needs only imperfectly. His vision of a spiritual coupling between mind and form—a union of kindred essences—required a higher degree of reciprocity than was allowed by any sexual model available to men of his culture. For a model of such reciprocity, he drew on a new image of pederastic love that he himself invented—"fully sensual in its resonance, but denying itself consummation, transmuting physical excitement into imaginative and intellectual energy" (Vlastos 1981, p. 22). Plato's model depicts a new kind of mutuality: a relation between two participating lovers rather than the traditional one between the passionate lover and the impassive beloved. In his model, desire and constraint are more equally distributed (see Halperin 1983). The perception of a youth's beauty evokes both love and reverence. In a man who has not yet been corrupted, who has not become accustomed to surrendering himself to sensuality, Eros inspires the soul; love enables him to make the transition from the "namesake," beauty on earth, to the absolute, the "celestial vision': "He receives through his eyes the emanation of beauty, by which the soul's plumage is fostered, and grows hot. . . . As the nourishing moisture falls upon it the stump of each feather under the whole surface of the soul swells and strives to grow from its root; for in its original state the soul was feathered all over. So now it is all in a state of ferment and throbbing" (*Phaedrus*, 251c).

Prompted by the perception of his own beauty, reflected in the eyes of his lover, the beloved in turn becomes aroused. The lover's Eros has evoked a counter-Eros, "the reflection of the love [the beloved] inspires" (*Phaedrus*, 255):

When their intimacy is established, . . . the "stream of

longing" sets in full flood towards the lover. Part of it enters
into him, but when his heart is full the rest brims over, and
as a wind or an echo rebounds from a smooth and solid
surface and is carried back to its point of origin, so the
stream of beauty returns once more to its source in the
beauty of the beloved. It enters in at his eyes, the natural
channel of communication with the soul, and reaching and
arousing the soul it moistens the passages from which the
feathers shoot and stimulates the growth of wings, and in
its turn the soul of the beloved is filled with love. (*Phaedrus*, 255)

Through such mutual reflection, each lover mirroring beauty to
the other, Eros both inspires and is inspired, sprouting wings in the
lovers, leading them, in tandem, ever higher toward absolute beauty
and truth. This erotic give-and-take, or mutual uplifting, does not
simply begin in physical desire and then leave it behind; physical
Eros, now reciprocated, remains its basic impetus. "Like his lover,
though less strongly, [the beloved] feels a desire to see, to touch, to
kiss him, and to share his bed. And naturally it is not long before
these desires are fulfilled in action" (*Phaedrus*, 255).

Plato, it seems, has discovered a model of sexual love that allows
for mutuality of desire without compromising the masculinity or
dignity of the beloved, without evoking a division into dominant and
subordinate roles, or the aggression that that entails. But such reciprocity is bought at a price, and the price is final sexual constraint.
Growth of the wings of the soul requires that actual consummation
be avoided. "If the higher elements in their minds prevail, and guide
them into a way of life which is strictly devoted to the pursuit of
wisdom, [the lovers] will pass their time on earth in happiness and
harmony; by subduing the part of the soul that contained the seeds
of vice and setting free that in which virtue has its birth they will
become masters of themselves and their souls will be at peace.
Finally, when this life is ended, their wings will carry them aloft"
(*Phaedrus*, 256). To this end, both partners must cooperate in opposing their lower impulses with "the moderating influence of modesty and reason" (*Phaedrus*, 256).

If not, if they should yield to temptation, the goal of knowledge
and absolute beauty will elude them. Consummation threatens the
return of the irrational and aggressive. In the Platonic model, knowl-

edge guided by love (the only true form of knowledge) requires a division not only of order from disorder but, equally, of erotic from aggressive. And however strongly Platonic Eros draws from bodily impulses, such division is finally possible only if those impulses are restrained. The status of the physical body remains that of the slave: subordinated, subdued, and excluded from the realm of philosophy. Only thus can Platonic knowledge enjoy the freedom of erotic mutuality.

It is important to note, however, that neither Plato's epistemology, his cosmology, nor his model of love is yet free of hierarchy. Everywhere, the eye, the soul, and the mind continue to look upward. And once again, the sexual model Plato employs serves as his paradigm; it contains the roots of this directionality, just as it illustrates the mutuality of the union of mind and Form. The beloved learns about love from his older and wiser lover, reflecting the other's eros, but to a lesser degree. The metaphor of mirrors is not meant to dissolve the intrinsic hierarchy of the relationship; rather it provides the means by which, within this hierarchy, the souls of both lover and beloved can be elevated. In relation to his *eromenos*, the *erastes* is a teacher, but in relation to knowledge, he is a student, looking always upward. By reflection, the beloved also learns to look upward. Together, they climb the "ladder of love," with the *erastes* always in the lead. It is first upon him that the obligation lies to make "his way upward by a right use of his feeling of love for boys" (*Symposium*, 211b), as Diotima explains:

> to begin with examples of beauty in this world, and using them as steps to ascend continually with that absolute beauty as one's aim, from one instance of physical beauty to two and from two to all, then from physical beauty to moral beauty, and from moral beauty to the beauty of knowledge, until from knowledge of various kinds one arrives at the supreme knowledge whose sole object is that absolute beauty, and knows at last what absolute beauty is. (*Symposium*, 211).

Plato's reconception of pederastic love, still hierarchical but free of domination, provides a metaphor for a form of knowledge that is erotic but that continues to suffer from its own internal inequalities. Just as it is not, finally, the beloved himself who is the object of love but rather the "image" of the Idea in him (see Vlastos 1981, p. 31), so it is not objects themselves of which one seeks understanding (or knowledge) but rather the Forms to which they point. Disregard for the embodied individual in and of itself pervades Plato's entire philosophical system as it describes his theory of love. Both are what Vlastos (1981, p. 30) calls "patently Ideocentric," seeking always to transcend the personal and particular. Excluding matter from his epistemology, and consummated sexuality from his definition of ideal Eros, does not leave Plato free to enjoy conceptual egalitarianism any more than banishing slaves from the polis would create the conditions for true democracy. In his politics as in his philosophy, the need for absolutism, however benevolent, remains.

In modern times, it is knowledge of material nature that preoccupies the natural philosopher—a preoccupation that excludes the Ideocentric emphasis of Platonic thought. But much of Plato's particular structuring of the intellectual and emotional landscape survives in this new conception. In particular, his division between the logical and the physical persists in the contemporary distinction between theoretical and experimental, as well as in the distinction between pure and applied. In the realm of theoretical physics, the modern physicist searches for the laws of nature; he seeks communion with the nexus of authority to which material nature is subservient. Nature as such remains divided between its material and logical essences, with the former described as "obeying" the latter. The internal structure of the theoretical world itself reflects a hierarchy similar to Plato's: the ideal of physics is the discovery of that single unifying law of nature from which all other laws can be derived. But in turning his attention to the physical world per se, the modern scientist must of necessity override Plato's stricture against inclusion of the physical; in doing so, he becomes a party to the aggression that Plato sought to avoid. The object of his study is no longer the Platonic Forms, a rarefied distillate of male sexuality, but material nature, the corporeal frame of female sexuality. Accordingly, the goals and even the methods of science change. Above all, the meaning of understanding changes. Consistent with the shift from male to female object, the goal of understanding is no longer primarily that of communion but of power: its aim is the domination of nature.

Modern science can thus be said to be following Plato's script, but without heeding his cautionary advice. In this script it appears inevitable that intercourse with physical nature evokes the domination and aggression appropriate to women and slaves. The language of modern science seems to bear out that inevitability, even in its invocation of a new set of images; homoerotic union is superseded by heterosexual conquest.

The most explicit source of the new imagery that emerges in the modern age is Francis Bacon, the man sometimes credited as the architect of modern science and perhaps best known for his celebration of the equation between knowledge and power. Bacon envisions science, not as a sublime love affair with the "essential nature of things," but as "a chaste and lawful marriage between Mind and Nature" (see chapt. 2).

The chastity of this marriage preserves the boundaries between Mind and Nature and, with the preservation of boundaries, secures the differences between the spouses: Nature, though law-bound, is devoid of mind. Chastity in Bacon's metaphor serves a function parallel to that of sexual constraint in Plato's—it preserves the disjunction between Eros and aggression—but now it protects the relationship of knower and known from Eros rather than from aggression. In neither vision is material nature (female for both Plato and Bacon) invited into a partnership of love: in one she is relegated to another realm, in the other she is seduced and conquered. Laid bare of her protective covering, exposed and penetrated even in her "innermost chambers," she is stripped of her power. Her secrets have become knowable. In the modern era the Furies have been not simply subdued but vanquished. But for all the differences between Bacon and Plato, what is perhaps most striking is the degree to which these changes follow directly—given the shift of attention to the study of material nature—from Plato's own segregation of logical and physical, erotic and aggressive. The hierarchical relation between mind and matter, and between male and female, that Bacon inherits from Plato's world view incorporates the very aggression that Plato had excluded. Although Bacon rejects Platonic doctrine, he remains faithful to the fundamental categories of his predecessor, and his vision of knowledge shares (in ways discussed in the next essay) some of the same ambiguities that arise in Plato.

It might be appropriate to conclude this essay by raising the

possibility of using alternative scripts or other sexual models in philosophical inquiry. In the end, Plato's definition of a new form of
pederastic love remained constrained by the cultural models available to him and the restrictions these imposed on acceptable forms
of desire in men. Given these restrictions, the only imaginable
model that might have offered an instance of reciprocal consummated sexuality, not automatically evoking aggression and inviting
domination, would have come either from female homosexual experience or from a female perspective on heterosexual experience.
The question suggested by this analysis is now obvious: How might
a different conception of sexuality, and of masculinity, modify the
conception of knowledge, of the relation of mind to nature, that Plato
bequeathed to us?

CHAPTER TWO

Baconian Science:
The Arts of
Mastery and Obedience

It has become common for social critics of modern science to assume that control and domination are basic to the scientific impulse. For such critics, the motives of scientific inquiry appear to have been defined by Bacon, for it was he who first and most vividly articulated the equation between scientific knowledge and power, who identified the aims of science as the control and domination of nature. Yet this view represents a particular reading of both science and Bacon.

Bacon's writings lend themselves easily to such a reading. Rejecting Plato's highly abstract and deeply erotic coupling of mind and form—indeed, rejecting all the major traditions that preceded him—Bacon's articulation of his vision was both provocative and aggressive. In viewing science as power, he thought he saw salvation. Indeed, the salvation of mankind was to be found in the very power of science. It thereby became the moral responsibility of men to assume and exercise that power. To his contemporaries, his vision of science as power and as salvation must have seemed fantastic on both counts. To us, he seems to have been prescient in the former and naive in the latter.

With the unfolding of history, Bacon's vision has taken on renewed but different interest. Public confidence and optimism have given way to anxiety, and some critics of science have begun to worry

A version of this chapter was originally published under the title "Baconian Science: A Hermaphroditic Birth" in *The Philosophical Forum*, vol. XI, no. 3, Spring 1980, pp. 299–307.

anew about aggression in the scientific impulse. But even as the practice of science has in fact become more explicitly and dramatically involved with power, the writings of scientists have become, if anything, more discreet and more qualifying in their descriptions of the nature of their enterprise. And so, to these critics, Bacon begins to take on the value not only of prescience but also of a bold and revealing honesty.

At the same time, his vision appears to others, particularly to the defenders of science, to be grossly distorted. It speaks more for the technologist than for the scientist, whose search it is said is as much for transcendence as it is for power. Bacon, it is asserted finally, was not really a scientist. Thus science is defended by dissociation from the unwelcome implications of Bacon's vision. That vision may well have been prescient for technology, but it is ultimately not relevant to pure science.

I will argue that Bacon has in fact provided us with a model that is truer to the spirit of the scientific impulse than is generally recognized by the defenders of science, and more complex than is recognized by many of its critics.

One of the ways in which the subtleties of Bacon's model find expression is through the sexual dialectic implicit in his metaphors. Bacon's vision was neither simply prophetic nor simply a misrepresentation of the emerging scientific enterprise. If we search his vivid metaphors with care, as I propose to do, paying particular attention to his use of gender, we find traces of a dialectic that is far more complicated and hence richer in meaning than either the critics or the defenders of science tend to assume. The sexual imagery in Bacon's language is neither as coherent nor as clearly articulated as Plato's, but Bacon nonetheless deserves examination here as a counterpart to Plato; he provided the language from which subsequent generations of scientists extracted a more consistent metaphor of lawful sexual domination.

Bacon's Metaphor

What was Bacon's vision? It was, without a doubt, of a science leading to the sovereignty, dominion, and mastery of man over nature, the "command of nature in action" (Anderson 1960, p. 19). It is in science that "human knowledge and human power meet in one" (ibid., p. 39), where man's native ambition for power finds its constructive, noble, and humane outlet. In distinguishing three kinds, or grades, of ambition, Bacon wrote:

> The first is of those who desire to extend their own power in their native country, a vulgar and degenerate kind. The second is of those who labor to extend the power and dominion of their country among men. This certainly has more dignity, though not less covetousness. But if a man endeavor to establish and extend the power and dominion of the human race itself over the universe, his ambition (if ambition it can be called) is without doubt both a more wholesome and a more noble thing than the other two. Now the empire of man over things depends wholly on the arts and sciences. For we cannot command nature except by obeying her. (ibid., p. 29)

Through science and art (that is, technology, or mechanical art), man can find the power to transform not so much the world as his relation to the world. The goal of science was, for Bacon, "the restitution and reinvesting of man to the sovereignty and power . . . which he had in his first state of creation" (Robertson 1905, p. 188). By what means, we need ask, and from what sources was science to acquire such power? And what was the shape it was to take?

Bacon's answer to these questions is given metaphorically—through his frequent and graphic use of sexual imagery. The invocation of gender and the use of sexual imagery are common enough in descriptions of nature, and perhaps for this reason Bacon's uses have not seemed especially noteworthy. It is important, however, to see how deeply Bacon's use of gender is implicated in his conception of mastery and domination. The fact that mastery and domination are, invariably, exercised over nature as "she" can hardly escape our attention, and indeed has not gone unnoticed (see, for example, Leiss 1972, p. 60). But, under scrutiny, it can be seen that Bacon's use of gender is not so simple. Less conspicuous but still visible is a more complex sexual dialectic—a dialectic whose complexities are not gratuitous but can be interpreted as parts of a description of the scientific impulse. To see the dialectical character of Bacon's imagery, and therefore to perceive the full meaning of his metaphor, it is useful to juxtapose some expressions, even well-worn expres-

sions, of that metaphor. Taken singly they may be familiar enough;
taken together they acquire new meaning.

"Let us establish" he wrote, "a chaste and lawful marriage between Mind and Nature" (quoted in Leiss 1972, p. 25); and again,
elsewhere, "My dear, dear boy, what I plan for you is to unite you
with things themselves in a chaste, holy and legal wedlock. And
from this association you will secure an increase beyond all the hopes
and prayers of ordinary marriages, to wit, a blessed race of Heroes
and Supermen" (Farrington 1951, p. 201). The word *things* here is
far from neutral. Elsewhere (even in the same work) he is more
explicit. It is Nature herself who is to be the bride, who requires
taming, shaping, and subduing by the scientific mind. "I am come
in very truth leading to you Nature with all her children to bind her
to your service and make her your slave" (ibid., p. 197). Elsewhere,
more gently, he writes: "I invite all such to join themselves, as true
sons of knowledge, with me, that passing by the outer courts of
nature, which numbers have trodden, we may find a way at length
into her inner chambers" (Anderson 1960, p. 36). Nature may be
coy, but she can be conquered, "For you have but to follow and as
it were hound nature in her wanderings, and you will be able, when
you like, to lead and drive her afterwards to the same place again"
(Spedding et al. 1869, 4: p. 296). The discipline of scientific knowledge, and the mechanical inventions it leads to, do not "merely exert
a gentle guidance over nature's course; they have the power to conquer and subdue her, to shake her to her foundations" (Spedding et
al. 1869, 5: p. 506). All of this is, however, in the service of truth.
In conquering and subduing, in shaking her to her foundations, we
do not so much transform Nature as reveal her, for "the nature of
things betrays itself more readily under the vexations of art" (meaning practical, or mechanical, art) "than in its natural freedom"
(Anderson 1960, p. 25).

But Bacon's formula is not simply aggressive—it is also responsive. He wrote: "For man is but the servant and interpreter of nature: what he does and what he knows is only what he has observed
of nature's order in fact or in thought; beyond this he knows nothing
and can do nothing. For the chains of causes cannot by any force be
loosed or broken, nor can nature be commanded except by being
obeyed" (Anderson 1960, p. 29). The aim of science is not to violate
but to master nature by following the dictates of the truly natural.

That is, it is "natural" to guide, shape, even hound, conquer, and subdue her—only in that way is the true "nature of things" revealed. It is here that the empirical side of Bacon's philosophy finds expression. Experiment expresses the spirit of action, of a "doing" devoted to "finding out." Science controls by following the dictates of nature, but these dictates include the requirement, even demand, for domination.

Not simple violation, or rape, but forceful and aggressive seduction leads to conquest. Alchemy was misguided, not in its aims, but in its methods. Rossi (1968, p. 105) sums up Bacon's interpretation of the myth of Erichthonious as follows: "The basic error of chemical and mechanical productions is not that they strive to dominate nature, but the method by which they attempt to do so; they rape Minerva instead of winning her over."[1]

Yet, the distinction between rape and conquest sometimes seems too subtle. There remains something of a puzzle. Nature is commanded by being obeyed, revealed by being enslaved, hounded, and vexed. The metaphor of seduction, even forceful and aggressive seduction, does not seem adequate to all the ambiguities that are intended. Indeed, in the context of so limited a metaphor, the ambiguities become contradictions. Science is to be aggressive yet responsive, powerful yet benign, masterful yet subservient, shrewd yet innocent, "as if the divine nature enjoyed the kindly innocence in such hide-and-seek, hiding only in order to be found, and with characteristic indulgence desired the human mind to join Him in this sport" (Farrington 1966, p. 92).[2]

Here, as nature becomes divine, the hunt turns to sport—kindly and innocent. At the same time, and surely not coincidentally, "she" becomes "he." The puzzle begins to dissolve as Bacon's metaphor expands. When nature becomes divine, not only does "she" become "he," but by implication as we shall see, the scientific mind becomes more nearly female. The sexual dialectic evident here begins to suggest a larger and richer metaphor for the scientific enterprise, a metaphor which is made generally more explicit in the fragments of a lesser known work of Bacon's entitled *Temporis Partus Masculus*, or *The Masculine Birth of Time*.

1. A different reading is provided in the next essay.
2. Also, in almost identical words, in *The Grand Instauration* (Anderson 1960, p. 15)

The Masculine Birth of Time

The fragments of this work, written in 1602 or 1603 and never published in Bacon's lifetime, have been translated by Farrington (1951), who says "it adds nothing to our knowledge of Bacon's teachings but it throws much light on his own emotional attitude to his work" (p. 193). The title is interpreted by Farrington as insinuating "that older science represented only a female off-spring, passive, weak, expectant, but now a son was born, active, virile, generative" (p. 194).

The key to the birth of a masculine, virile science is to be found in the cleansing of the human mind of "false preconceptions," so as to facilitate its receptivity. In the first chapter he asks, "Do you suppose that men's minds offer flawless polished surfaces for the reception of the true native rays of real things? In fact every avenue to every mind is beset and blocked by the darkest idols, or false preconceptions are deeprooted or burned in" (p. 194).

The crucial concepts in this image of Mind are reception and submission—unobstructed receptivity to the "true native rays of real things." Only then can "the unlocking of the paths of sense and the unkindling of a greater light in Nature" come about.[3] The imagery of submission is in noteworthy contrast to the male imagery of mastery that Bacon typically used to describe the relation of mind to nature.

What is sought in this passage is the proper stance for mind necessary to ensure the reception of truth and the conception of science. To receive God's truth, the mind must be pure and clean, submissive and open. Only then can it give birth to a masculine and virile science. That is, if the mind is pure, receptive, and submissive in its relation to God, it can be transformed by God into a forceful, potent, and virile agent in its relation to nature. Cleansed of contamination, the mind can be impregnated by God and, in that act, virilized: made potent and capable of generating virile offspring in its union with Nature.

---

3. In his preface to the *History of Winds*, twenty years later, Bacon explicitly equates the "chastity" of the philosopher's relation to Nature with the cleansing of the mind: "Men are to be entreated again and again . . . that they should humbly and with a certain reverence draw near to the book of Creation . . . that on it they should meditate, and that then washed and clean they should in chastity and integrity turn them from opinion" (in Farrington 1964, p. 54).

The transformation of mind from female to male is made explicit in the structure of this work. The first part is a prayer addressed to God, in the voice of a supplicant. The remainder, and body, of the work is cast in the voice of the mature scientist addressing a son, his virile offspring. Henceforth, Nature becomes indubitably female: the object of actions. It is here that we read, "I am come in very truth leading to you Nature with all her children to bind her to your service and make her your slave." In the same passage, he further bequeaths to this son the heritage of "my only earthly wish, namely to stretch the deplorable narrow limits of man's dominion over the universe to their promised bounds" (p. 197).

Notice the God-like voice in which Bacon now addresses his son and heir. The son, in turn, is invited to assume the posture of supplicant: "Take heart, then, my son, and give yourself to me, so that I may restore you to yourself" (p. 201). Restoration begins with clearing the son's mind of the influence of "sham philosophers," of those who "debauch our minds" (p. 197). To this end the bulk of the work is devoted.

Aristotle, Plato, Galen, Hippocrates successfully come in for a most flagrant debunking. They convey false teachings that block and impede the mind's true receptivity to "the true native rays of real things." Bacon's language is strong. "It was in Aristotle's bosom that were bred and nurtured those crafty triflers . . . the darksome idols from some subterranean cave" (p. 198). Plato is denounced for giving out "the falsehood that truth is, as it were, the native inhabitant of the human mind and need not come in from outside to take up its abode there" (p. 198). Galen is charged with "the malicious intention of lessening human power" (p. 199).

These were the men who gave rise to the older science—the science that Farrington says, in Bacon's view, "represented only a female offspring" in contrast with the "masculine birth" that Bacon now heralds. Yet the terms of their debunking express the same complex duality or dialectic we have already seen. The teachings of the ancients are dangerous not simply because they are unproductive, but also because they discourage receptivity. Plato taught false self-sufficiency; his doctrine left no space for the need of truth to enter the mind from without. The grievous error of the ancients, concludes Farrington, was that "they sought to create the universe out of the human mind. This presumptuous usurpation of the prerogative of the Creator was punished by the curse of barrenness (p. 202). But not just barrenness, which is a female imperfection— also impotence and the inability to sire virile offspring. The errors of the ancients were more various than this, but they had in common the net effect of breeding impotence, of "lessening human power," of retarding the birth of the true and masculine science that, Bacon says, "is to be sought from the light of nature, not the darkness of antiquity" (p. 200). The causes of past impotence and feminization in Bacon's vision are as complex as the sources of future potency.

Concluding the work, Bacon warns the neophyte scientist that the task of cleansing the mind is a difficult one, and requires a long and faithful apprenticeship. Bacon offers himself as guide and leader, promising thereby to "restore" the youth to himself, to lead him into a marriage that will yield "Heroes and Supermen," to prepare him for his rightful ascendancy.

Interpretation and Conclusion

The metaphor that Bacon employs to articulate his vision for the birth of science is now seen to be suffused with overtones of considerable subtlety. Behind the overt insistence on the virility and masculinity of the scientific mind lies a covert assumption and acknowledgment of the dialectical, even hermaphroditic, nature of the "marriage between Mind and Nature." This recognition can stand on its own, for Bacon's imagery reveals itself. It is, however, possible to make a further interpretation.

The two-sided character of Bacon's metaphor can be seen as expressing not only the dual nature of the scientific venture, simultaneously receptive and potent, but also a ubiquitous fantasy of childhood sexuality. The virilization of the scientist, and of the child as well, is acquired as a gift received from the father. This gift permits the scientist to father "Heroes and Supermen"; it provides him with the capacity, as it were, to give birth to himself. It is this aspect of Bacon's metaphor, and of the child's fantasy, that reveals the implicitly bisexual character of the oedipal project. Freud wrote, in *The Ego and the Id*:

> The simple Oedipus complex is by no means its commonest form, but rather represents a simplification or schematiza-

tion which, to be sure, is often enough adequate for practical purposes. Closer study usually discloses the more complete Oedipus complex, which is twofold, positive and negative, and is due to the bisexuality originally present in children: that is to say, a boy has not merely an ambivalent attitude towards his father and an affectionate object-relation to-wards his mother, but at the same time he also behaves like a girl and displays an affectionate feminine attitude to his father and a corresponding hostility and jealousy towards his mother. (1927, p. 220)

The impulse to identify oneself simultaneously with the mother and the father finds exquisitely face-saving and economical expression in what Freud described as the oedipal boy's "wish to be the father of himself" (1950, 4, p. 201). Its economy is achieved by condensation, and budding masculine pride is sustained by elision. In fact that fantasy, by virtue of its compression of so many conflicting wishes, reveals the poetic genius of the young boy's unconscious. Through condensation and elision, it allows for the subterranean survival of wishes no longer deemd acceptable, wishes regarded as feminine. Thus, in identifying himself with the race of fathers who can give birth, the young boy can simultaneously assert his independence and safeguard the earlier and conflicting wish for identification with the mother; in presuming to father himself, he satisfies his wish for omnipotent self-sufficiency.

The Baconian metaphor, in condensing the dual impulse to appropriate and deny the maternal, seems to resemble the boy's oedipal ambitions. As such it represents a bypass, a compensation for and a way of doing without the mother. Omnipotence is secured by an identification with the father which allows simultaneously for the appropriation and denial of the feminine. Both the child and science can now enter the man's world.

In the context of this interpretation, the sexual aggressivity of Bacon's imagery begins to assume a somewhat defensive quality. What is most immediately conspicuous in that imagery is its denial of the feminine as subject—a denial often taken to be generally characteristic of the scientific endeavor. But, when we examine the imagery more carefully, we find, behind that simple denial, a prior cooptation of the female mode—a cooptation which, given the initial impulse toward denial, necessitates an ever more urgent and aggressive repudiation. That is to say, the aggressively male stance of Bacon's scientist could, and perhaps now should, be seen as driven by the need to deny what all scientists, including Bacon, privately have known, namely, that the scientific mind must be, on some level, a hermaphroditic mind.

It is in this sense that Bacon's metaphor, taken in its entirety, becomes richer and more complete, and, as such, provides a more accurate description of the scientific impulse. This description may well represent a version of the oedipal project, but one that retains all the bisexual implications of that project intact. In contemporary times, the explicit role of God has disappeared, and the scientific fantasy has become more self-contained. Where Bacon was able to parcel out the dual aspects of the scientific mind by assigning one of these functions to the relation of mind to God, or to divine nature, and the other to Nature, contemporary scientists cannot. For most scientists today, there is only one Nature, and only one mind.[4] The scientist himself has assumed the procreative function that Bacon reserved for God: his mind is now a single entity, both phallus and womb. However, his kinship with Bacon survives in his simultaneous appropriation and denial of the feminine.

> and dream of masculine
> filiation, dream of God the father
> emerging from himself
> in his son,—and
> no mother then.
>
> HÉLÈNE CIXOUS, "Sorties" (1981)

---

4. This claim now seems to me too simple; see especially chap. 3.

CHAPTER THREE

Spirit and Reason at the Birth of Modern Science

No one has such power but he who has cohabited with
the elements.

AGRIPPA, quoted in Yates (1969, p. 136)

Magic has power to experience and fathom things
which are inaccessible to human reason. For magic is
a great secret wisdom, just as reason is a great public
folly. Therefore it would be desirable and good for the
doctors of theology to know something about it and
to understand what it actually is, and cease unjustly
and unfoundedly to call it witchcraft.

PARACELSUS, ed. Jacobi (1958, p. 137)

The institutionalization of modern science in seventeenth-century
England is a familiar subject for historians of science, and a growing
body of research has illuminated the many social and political factors
that inform the philosophical debates attending that critical moment.[1] But if modern science evolved in, and helped to shape, a
particular social and political context, by the same token it evolved
in conjunction with, and helped to shape, a particular ideology of
gender. I argue that we cannot properly understand the development
of modern science without attending to the role played by metaphors
of gender in the formation of the particular set of values, aims, and
goals embodied in the scientific enterprise. In this essay I hope to
show that attention to the language of sex and gender—so prevalent

1. See, e.g., Christopher Hill, 1972; Charles Webster, 1975; Margaret Jacob,
1976; J. R. Jacob, 1977; and the works of P. M. Rattansi (1963, 1968) and Allen G.
Debus (1972, 1978).

43

in early scientific discourse—casts a new light on this crucial moment in the history of science and helps to explain certain otherwise anomalous features of that history. In particular, it suggests gender ideology as a crucial mediator between the birth of modern science and the economic and political transformations surrounding that birth. Our inquiry confirms that neither the equations between mind, reason, and masculinity, nor the dichotomies between mind and nature, reason and feeling, masculine and feminine, are historically invariant. Even though the roots of both the equations and the dichotomies may be ancient, the seventeenth century witnessed a marked polarization of all the terms involved—with consequences as crucial for science as for our understanding of gender.

To make this case, I want to focus on certain intellectual debates immediately preceding the founding of the Royal Society. Numerous authors have documented the complexity of the society's intellectual origins, warning us of the difficulties of retrospectively applying contemporary conceptions of science to that earlier time. In the seventeenth century, although natural philosophers may have been united in their enthusiasm for a "new science," they were hardly united in their visions of what such a "new science" might mean. But even though no simple categories suffice to describe the variety of interests and beliefs that prevailed, it is possible to describe the intellectual history of that period schematically, in terms of two competing philosophies, hermetic and mechanical: two visions of a "new science" that often competed even within the minds of individual thinkers. In the hermetic tradition, material nature was suffused with spirit; its understanding accordingly required the joint and integrated effort of heart, hand, and mind. By contrast, the mechanical philosophers sought to divorce matter from spirit, and hand and mind from heart.[2] The line between these two traditions was, however, as yet only sketchily drawn. I begin with a brief description of the intellectual and political climate that surrounded these debates and informed distinctions that emerged more sharply in subsequent years.

---

2. An excellent account of the transition from premechanical "new philosophies" in the hermetic tradition to mechanical philosophy in seventeenth-century England is provided by P. M. Rattansi (1968).

Contending Visions of the New Science

The intellectual climate of seventeenth-century England was characterized by a heightened interest in the pursuit of experimental knowledge of material nature—knowledge that would serve the glory of God as well as the interests of man—and by an associated rebellion against the hold that ancient philosophers had over men's minds. Close to the center of this unrest stood the contemporary representatives of the hermetic tradition, the Renaissance alchemists. Inspired by the works of Paracelsus in the previous century, seventeenth-century alchemists were principally concerned with the transformative, especially curative, powers of chemically prepared medicines; their pursuit of the transmutation of base metal into gold was largely emblematic. Although they foresaw a universal science capable of explaining the entire natural world, their major successes and influence lay in chemistry and medicine. It was as evident to these Paracelsians as it was to Bacon that the mantles of Aristotle and Galen needed to be discarded. But for the alchemists, the reigning medical orthodoxy and a moribund university curriculum were special targets of attack. John Webster, a Paracelsian, a surgeon, and a chaplain in the Parliamentary Army, advocated that

> youth may not be idely trained up in notions, speculations and verbal disputes, but may learn to inure their hands to labour, and put their fingers to the furnaces . . . that they may not grow proud with the brood of their own brains, but truly taught by manual operation, and ocular experiment, that so they may not be sayers, but doers, not idel speculators, but painful operators; that they may not be Sophisters and Philosophers, but . . . true Natural Magicians, that walk not in the external circumference, but in the center of nature's hidden secrets, which can never come to pass, unless they have Laboratories as well as Libraries, and work in the fire, better than build Castles in the air. (1654, p. 106)

Interest in Paracelsian philosophy reached a high point in England during the 1640s and 1650s—the period of the Puritan Revolution. The emphasis on illumination derived from direct experience (available to anyone who pursues the art) accorded well with the religious and political ambitions of the times. The works of Paracelsus were translated into English, widely distributed, and referred to everywhere.[3] The principles of hermetic philosophy captured the imagination of many thinkers, including the members of the Oxford Group (a precursor of the Royal Society) but were perhaps especially attractive to political and religious radicals. During the 1650s, however, such leading intellectuals as Robert Boyle, Walter Charleton, and Henry More shifted their allegiances, abandoned their earlier hermetic sympathies, and became strong proponents of the newly published mechanical viewpoints of Gassendi and Descartes. At the end of the 1650s, a fiercely bitter campaign was mounted against the alchemical "enthusiasts" by a number of the leading moderate churchmen—at least some of whom were soon to become founding members of the Royal Society. After 1660 the scales had tipped; by the late 1670s the rivalry was over. The Royal Society, established in 1662 and marking the institutionalization of the new science, was seen by many of its members as a realization of the Baconian program (see, for example, Rossi 1968, pp. xiii, 218). Although a number of its members continued in an attempt to reconcile some features of hermeticism with the new philosophy, the society had little room for publicly avowed "enthusiasts."[4]

In attempting to explain the dramatic upsurge of interest in alchemy at the beginning of this period and its equally dramatic demise at the end, a number of scholars have focused on two features: the "anti-rationalism" of the alchemists and their radical religious heterodoxy. Rattansi, for example, argues that

> people of diverse views were swayed for a time by the feeling that, since religious and political disputes had . . . plunged the country into the horrors of civil war, man must abandon that faculty of reasoning, which had generated those divisions, and throw himself upon the supposedly uncontroversial testimony of the spirit within. (1963, p. 26)

3. Brian Easlea (1980, p. 131) remarks that, in the 1640s, "more Paracelsian and alchemical works [were] translated into English than in the preceding 100 years."

4. Elias Ashmole was an exception; but, as Van den Daele (1977, p. 41) remarks, the more radical and far more influential Samuel Hartlib was never proposed as one of the Fellows of the Royal Society, nor does his name appear in their official records or history.

But, he continues,

> by the 1650s, the doctrine of "private illumination" so widely invoked at the beginning of the Puritan Revolution, was proving a deep embarrassment and a source of danger to the authority established in Church and State after the overthrow of monarchy. . . . Those who keenly sensed that danger strove to curtail, as drastically as possible, the claims of sectarians who alleged divine inspiration. (1963, p. 29)

The forces of rebellion unleashed during the 1640s and 1650s prompted a widespread reaction of conservatism among the intellectual elite. Alchemy was one target of this reaction; the social reformism of the early Baconians was another. A more reductionist experimental science, with neither social nor educational ambitions, seemed the safest course. Frances Yates (1978, pp. 188–90), for example, writes,

> As the natural philosophers moved towards the consummation of the Royal Society, they had to be very careful. . . . A permanent Society for the advancement of natural science had arrived. . . . [But] it was very restricted in its aims compared with earlier movements. It did not envisage the advancement of science within a reformed society, within a universal reformation of the whole world. The Fellows of the Royal Society were not concerned with healing the sick, and that gratis, nor with schemes for the reform of education.

They were, as Van den Daele adds, "seeking a niche within society, not the reform of that society" (1977, p. 41).

However, there is another related theme, distinguishing between alternative visions of the "new science," that has not been adequately discussed by historians of science. Alongside, and interlaced with, the economic, social, political, and intellectual upheavals of this period, historians have recently begun to document a subtle but significant transformation in conceptions of and attitudes toward sexuality and gender roles. This transformation is reflected with particular clarity in the sexual language pervading much of seventeenth-century discourse on what a "new science" should look like. The

language of these debates calls our attention to a division that antic-
ipated but still remained relevant to the split between hermetical
and mechanical philosophies. In particular, an analysis of this language introduces a cut between Francis Bacon and the Paracelsians—a cut which, I suggest, becomes of crucial significance in
postrevolutionary debates.

A problematic and ambiguous figure in the history of science, Bacon
remains of interest to us primarily because of the force of his vision.
He foresaw the coming into being of a science and technology (a
"Masculine Birth of Time") with the power to transform man's relation to nature. His central metaphor—science as power, a force
virile enough to penetrate and subdue nature—has provided an image that permeates the rhetoric of modern science. Renaissance
alchemists also sought power in their vision of science, but for them
power had a quite different meaning. The difference between these
two conceptions of power, and of science, can readily be seen in the
opposing sexual metaphors underlying their visions.
    If the root image for Bacon was a "chaste and lawful marriage
between Mind and Nature" that will "bind [Nature] to [man's] service and make her [his] slave" (Farrington 1951, p. 197), the emphasis
was on constraint, on the disjunction between mind and nature, and
ultimately on domination. By contrast, the root image of the alchemists was coition, the conjunction of mind and matter, the merging
of male and female. As Bacon's metaphoric ideal was the virile super-
man, the alchemist's ideal was the hermaphrodite. Whereas Bacon
sought domination, the alchemists asserted the necessity of allegorical, if not actual, cooperation between male and female. Power for
them was to be achieved through "cohabit[ing] with the elements"
(Agrippa, from Yates, 1969, p. 136).
    Indeed, the hermaphrodite and the marital couple provide the
basic images of the writings and iconography that the alchemists left
behind. In depicting hermaphroditic union, sexual union, or simply
the collaborative effort of man and woman, their graphic images
represent the conjunction, or marriage, of male and female principles
that was central to hermetic philosophy. Alchemical texts make explicit and extensive use of marriage as the metaphor for the principle
of harmony underlying the relation of sun to moon, of form to sub-

stance, of spirit to matter, of mind to nature—in short underlying
the alchemists' view of the cosmos.[5] Consider, for example, the language of Giambattista della Porta, writing in the sixteenth century:

> The whole world is knit and bound within itself: for the
> world is a living creature, everywhere both male and fe-
> male, and the parts of it do couple together . . . by reason
> of their mutual love. (quoted in Merchant 1980, p. 104)

Similarly, Paracelsus writes:

> A man without a woman is not whole, only with a woman
> is he whole. . . . both are of earth and form together one
> whole. . . . Similarly, man and remedy . . . together form
> one whole. . . . In this sense, the disease desires its wife,
> that is, the medicine. . . . Both must be united to form a
> harmonious whole, just as in the case of man and woman.
> (ed. Jacobi 1951, pp. 73–74)

The notion that "disease desires its wife" is reminiscent of Aristotle's
view that matter "longs" for form, but alchemical writings suggest a
principle of symmetry (one might almost say of equality) between
male and female principles that is quite different from the Aristo-
telian view. Elsewhere Paracelsus writes:

> When the seed is received in the womb, nature combines
> the seed of the man and the seed of the woman. Of the two
> seeds the better and stronger will form the other according
> to its nature. . . . The seed from the man's brain and that
> from the woman's brain together make only one brain; but
> the child's brain is formed according to the one which is
> the stronger of the two, and it becomes like this seed but
> never completely like it. (p. 27)

5. I am indebted to Michele Le Doeuff for calling my attention to a crucial
ambiguity here. Just as the verb *to marry* can mean both to join husband and wife
(as, for example, a priest does) and to join oneself to another, so marriage can serve
as a metaphor for the wedding of different aspects of nature or for the wedding of
mind to nature. I suggest that for the alchemists it does both—at times more in the
first sense than in the second—but almost always without a clear distinction between
the two meanings.

A hundred years later, Thomas Vaughan, a major proponent of the Paracelsian tradition, argued that the object of the alchemist's search is not gold or silver: "In plain terms, . . . it is the seed of the greater animal, the seed of heaven and earth, our most secret and miraculous hermaphrodite." He explains:

> As . . . the conjunction of male and female tends towards a fruit and propagation becoming the nature of each, so in man himself that interior and secret association of male and female, to wit the copulation of male and female soul, is appointed for the production of fitting fruit of Divine Life. . . . marriage is a comment on life, a mere hieroglyphic or outward representation of our inward vital composition. For life is nothing else but an union of male and female principles, and he that perfectly knows this secret knows the mysteries of marriage—both spiritual and natural. . . . Marriage is no ordinary trivial business, but in a moderate sense sacramental. It is a visible sign of our invisible union to Christ. (1650a, p. 34)

Elsewhere, Vaughan elaborates his reasons for regarding marriage, and the union of male and female principles, as the fundamental sign of God in nature:

> There is in every star and in this elemental world a certain principle which is "the Bride of the Sun." These two in their coition do emit semen, which seed is carried in the womb of Nature. But the ejection of it is performed invisibly and in a sacred silence . . . a thing done in private between particular males and females; but how much more—think you—between the two universal natures. Know therefore that it is impossible for you to extract or receive any seed from the sun without this feminine principle, which is the Wife of the Sun. . . . Know then for certain that the magician's sun and moon are two universal peers, male and female, a king and queen regents. . . . These two are adequate to the whole world and co-extended through the whole universe. The one is not without the other. (1650b, p. 94)

"Two universal peers, male and female, a king and queen regents" represent the structure of the cosmos; the relation of all things to one another, including even our own understanding of natural phenomena, is reflected in the conjugal relation of the royal couple, above all in their sexual intimacy. Our knowledge itself is evidence—signed in the marital union—of our "invisible union to God."

At times, Vaughan's rhetoric may appear more similar to Bacon's than opposed to it, and this similarity has been emphasized by Easlea (1980). Both, it is true, are engaged in the search for the method of true knowing, the means by which one can penetrate the "innermost core of Nature."[6] For both, the proper path is defined by "experiment" rather than by theory. Vaughan writes:

> I advise them therefore to use their hands, not their fancies, and to change their abstractions into extractions; for verily as long as they lick the shell in this fashion and pierce not experimentally into the centre of things they can do not otherwise than they have done. They cannot know things substantially.

But an important difference distinguishes his vision from that of the mechanical philosophers. He goes on to explain:

> Have a care lest you misconceive me. I speak not in this place of the Divine Spirit, but I speak of a certain Art by which a particular spirit may be united to the universal, and Nature by consequence may be strangely exalted and multiplied. . . . I may exhort you to magic in the magician's phrase: "HEAR WITH THE UNDERSTANDING OF THE HEART." (1650a, p. 77)

This difference was not missed by many, and especially not by Henry More, the Cambridge Neo-platonist, early champion of

---

6. Such similarity in rhetoric has led Easlea to emphasize the continuity between alchemy and modern science. Easlea argues that both traditions shared the same phallic dream: to expose, pierce, penetrate—and thereby to dominate—Nature. My purpose here, by contrast, is to emphasize the difference between the two traditions, without, however, denying the very real overlaps and similarities that Easlea (and others, see, e.g., n. 9) has observed. Notwithstanding the difference in emphasis, and sometimes in interpretation, Easlea's work covers (far more extensively) much of the same ground I have attempted to cover here.

Cartesian philosophy, and soon to be Fellow of the Royal Society. More published two virulent attacks on Paracelsian enthusiasm in 1650 and 1656, in which he warned against the kind of "genius who loves to be tumbling and trying tricks with. . . . Matter (which they call making Experiments) when *desire of knowledge* has so heated it [genius]" that it is subject to the "wildest hallucinations possible" (1656, p. 36). More fears that such a pursuit makes a man "first fanatical; and then Atheisticall and sensuall" (quoted in Easlea 1980, p. 133). His charges to Vaughan in particular are more specific, and more damning: "Thou has not laid Madam Nature so naked as though supposest, only thou hast, I am afraid, dream't uncleanly, and so hast polluted so many sheets of paper with thy Nocturnall Canundrums [*sic*]" (1650, p. 57).[7]

In sympathy with More's attitudes and in contrast to the vision of the alchemists, Henry Oldenburg, Secretary of the Royal Society, announced a few years later that the intention of that society was "to raise a Masculine Philosophy . . . whereby the Mind of Man may be ennobled with the knowledge of Solid Truths" (Easlea 1980, p. 70). Joseph Glanvill, one of the chief propagandists of the Royal Society, writes in a similar vein. Whereas Paracelsus had written that "the art of medicine is rooted in the heart"—that one "discovers the curative virtues of remedies" by "true love" (ed. Jacobi 1951, p. 73)—Glanvill instead warned against the "power our *affections* have over our so easily seducible Understandings" (1661, p. 117). He writes: "That Jove himself cannot be *wise* and in *Love*; may be understood in a larger sense, than Antiquity meant it": [W]here the

---

7. The language of uncleanliness and pollution in More's attack is indicative not only of the strength of his feeling but, more generally, of a larger shift both in attitudes toward sexuality and (as Katherine Hayles has pointed out to me) in the very understanding of what is "lawful." The sexual passion that had earlier been (and was still, to the alchemists) consonant with sacramental union was now increasingly seen as unlawful and unclean. What is at issue here, in part at least, is the question of how concupiscence can be reconciled with rationality. More is speaking to a growing sentiment that defines all that is not strictly rational as "wildest hallucination," "unclean," "polluted" and finally, unlawful. Hayles (private communication) suggests further that this shift is crucially linked to the establishment of patrimonial lineage, legitimacy, and inheritance. Thus the meaning of chastity in Bacon's "chaste and lawful marriage" needs to be understood in the context of the definition of "lawful" that allows for succession and accumulation—finally, for inheritable progress. In ways that the alchemical tradition did not permit, "dwarfs" could now "stand on the shoulders of giants."

Will[8] or *Passion* hath the casting voyce, the case of *Truth* is *desparate*. . . . The *Woman* in us, still prosecutes a deceit, like that begun in the *Garden*; and our *Understandings* are wedded to an *Eve*, as fatal as the *Mother* of our *miseries*" (1661, pp. 117–18). In short, he concludes, truth has no chance when "the *Affections* wear the breeches and the *Female* rules" (p. 135).

The issue under dispute may have had little direct relation to the realpolitik of sexual domination, but it appears to have had a great deal to do with the evaluation of what was regarded as feminine, particularly with the place of feminine traits in the new definitions of knowledge. It can safely be said that none of the participants in this dispute was addressing issues of actual relations between the sexes; on the other hand, I suggest that they *were* concerned with the definition of gender, especially of what it meant to be a man, and what it meant to "raise a Masculine philosophy." The alchemists were not feminists. In many ways, they shared in the general contempt for women of their time. But for them, women's procreative powers remained a matter of reverence, awe, and even envy.[9] Paracelsus wrote: "How can one be an enemy of woman—whatever she may be? The world is peopled with her fruits, and that is why God lets her live so long, however loathsome She may be" (ed. Jacobi 1951, p. 26). Indeed, woman's capacity to give birth was a sign of Divine benediction. Contempt, for the alchemists, was countered by a firm conviction of the symbolic equality of male and female before God. As they saw it, the "Image of God" was engraved in woman just as it was in man (ibid., p. 266). Accordingly, participation in hermaphroditic union, be it in the soul of man or in the universal essence, was a Godly aspiration.

Francis Bacon himself was in many ways a transitional figure between hermetic and mechnical views; he shared with the alchemists both a distrust of the intellect "working upon itself" and an interest in social reform. But his attitude toward gender and sexuality, expressed in his vision of science as a "Masculine Birth of

8. *Will* was commonly used in the seventeenth century to denote carnal desire or appetite (see Oxford English Dictionary; also Eric Partridge 1969, pp. 218–19). I am grateful to N. Katherine Hayles for pointing this meaning out to me.

9. Sally Allen and Joanna Hubbs (1980) make an important point when they argue for the desire, evident in alchemical writings, to coopt the female procreative role. A similar desire can be discerned in Bacon's writings as well (see chap. 2).

Time" that will issue in a "blessed race of Heroes and Supermen"—
a force that can "hound," "conquer and subdue Nature," "shake her
to her foundations," "storm and occupy her castles and
strongholds"[10]—retrospectively marks him as a kinsman of the later
Fellows of the Royal Society. The founding fathers of modern science
rejected some elements of Bacon's thought and often retained at
least a covert interest in alchemy (Newton is a notable example), but
their break with their hermetic forebears was quite sharp in one
respect: they embraced the patriarchal imagery of Baconian science
and rejected the more participatory and erotic language of the alchemists. A recurrent token of this is their Baconian use of "masculine"
as an epithet for privileged, productive knowledge. As Thomas Sprat
(1667) explains in his defense of the Royal Society, "the *Wit* that is
founded on the *Arts* of mens' hands is masculine and durable." In
true Baconian idiom, Joseph Glanvill adds that the function of science is to discover "the ways of *captivating Nature*, and making her
subserve our *purposes*" (Easlea 1980, p. 214). The goal of the new
science is not metaphysical intercourse but domination, not the
union of mind and matter but the establishment of the "Empire of
Man over Nature." The triumph of those who have been generally
grouped together as "mechanical philosophers" represented a decisive defeat of the view of nature and woman as Godly, and of a
science which would accordingly have guaranteed to both at least a
modicum of respect.[11]

10. See notes to chap. 2.
11. In her extensive study of the changing images of nature reflected in the
scientific revolution (*The Death of Nature*, 1980), Carolyn Merchant has argued that
the central thrust of the scientific revolution was to take woman out of nature, leaving
nature as pure machine. Examining the contest between the alchemists and the
mechanists gives us a slightly different reading. Rather than taking woman out of
nature, one might almost say that the real impact of the scientific revolution was, in
a single move, to take God out of woman *and* out of material nature. In "A Free
Inquiry into the Vulgar Notion of Nature" (ed. Shaw, 1738, vol. 2, p. 107), Robert
Boyle made an impassioned plea against "the veneration men commonly have for
what they call nature, [which] has obstructed and confined the empire of man over
the inferior creatures." Among other recommendations, he urged that, "instead of
using the word nature, taken for either a goddess, or a kind of semi-deity; we wholly
reject, or very seldom employ it" (pp. 110–11). The effect of such "secularization" of
nature was to leave the equation between nature and woman intact: both were now
part mechanical and part demonic. In this argument, nature—still female—emerges
as pure machine only after the belief in witchcraft subsides.

The Decline of Renaissance Alchemy

It is not the purpose of this essay to review the scientific merits of alchemical research but rather to focus on some of the ideological issues that contributed to the demise of alchemy. If, from our present vantage point, the scientific successes of alchemy are thought to have been minimal,[12] it needs to be added that, in the mid-seventeenth century, the very notion of scientific success in the modern sense was as yet unformulated. Indeed, as van den Daele (1977, p. 39) writes:

> The historical choice between the variants of the new science cannot adequately be described as a process of cognitively controlled selection. Prior to 1660 there was no discernible tradition belonging to the positive experimental philosophy within which its superiority over other concepts of the new science could have been demonstrated. Nor was there, prior to the founding of the Royal Society, any institutional forum in which evaluations of the particular sciences could have visibly taken place. Moreover, the criteria according to which the primacy of positive science was established were only made cognitively binding through the institutionalization of this science. Controversies regarding the various concepts of science were often a mixture of, in the modern sense, "scientific" and politico-religious arguments.

In the light of recent scholarship, the discrepancy between this description and the traditional portrait of the origins of modern science is no longer surprising. As Charles Webster (1975, p. 494) has put it:

> Conclusions about the independence of scientific activity in the seventeenth century are based not on the impartial and exhaustive examination of evidence, but are rather dictated by the requirements of current ideology, and describe not the relationship which actually existed, but the relationship

12. The scientific value and influence of alchemical research have been subject to considerable reexamination in recent literature. See, e.g., Allen G. Debus (ed.) 1972, and Dobbs 1975.

which it is felt ought to have existed on the basis of present-day opinion about the methodology of science.

The inadequacy of a contemporary perspective for judging the relevant issues in the competition between hermetical and mechanical philosophies is perhaps nowhere better revealed than in the debate between certain proponents of the two schools over witchcraft—one of the more perplexing incidents in the history of the birth of modern science. This debate, between Joseph Glanvill and Henry More of the Royal Society on one side, and John Webster, the radical Protestant and chemical physician, on the other, was a pivotal event in the contest that raged throughout the 1660s and 1670s over the proper definition of the new science; it was also the most exhaustive debate on witchcraft in Restoration England. Both for its curiosity and for its importance, it is worth reviewing in some detail.[13]

Science and Witches

In 1664 a justice of the peace named Robert Hunt uncovered a coven of witches in Somersetshire; he sent a copy of his deposition to his friend Joseph Glanvill, complaining of the skepticism of the local gentry. Glanvill rose to the task, and, in 1666, published a work entitled *Some Philosophical Considerations Touching Witchcraft and Witches*. The popularity of this work was such that Glanvill expanded the fourth edition, which he published under the title *A Blow at Modern Saduccism*. In this work he transcribed in detail numerous accounts of "Demoniak Tumults," including a report of his own private investigations. His purpose was to demonstrate the reality of these phenomena and to map the "land of Spirits." He wrote: "For we know not anything of the world we live in, but by experiment and the Phenomena; and there is the same way of speculating immaterial nature, by extraordinary Events and Apparitions . . . were there a cautious, and Faithful History made of those certain and uncommon appearances." As a scientist, he argued, one had to put on the "Garb of the Naturalist" to investigate the world of the spirits, the reality of which was proved by the "attestation of

13. For an excellent and comprehensive discussion of this debate, see Jobe 1981.

Thousands of Eye and Ear witnesses, and those not of the easily deceivable Vulgar only, but of wise and grave Discerners; and that when no Interest could oblige them to agree together in a common Lye" (1668, pp. 115–17, cited by Jobe, p. 347).

Glanvill's widely read, eminently reasonable, and persuasive testimony was followed by Meric Casaubon's "A Treatis Proving Spirits, Witches and Supernatural Operations" in 1672, equally popular and equally persuasive. The Puritan divine, John Webster, alarmed by the influence of these works, countered in 1677 with a massive refutation, "The Displaying of Supposed Witchcraft." Webster argued that it was blasphemy to attribute the abstruse wonders and works of God to the Devil, and further cautioned that the Devil's power lay in mental temptation and not in physical effects. Henry More, a veteran from his debates with Thomas Vaughan, joined in, charging that Webster denied the reality of witchcraft in order to conceal his own alliance with witches and his affiliation with the Devil. In a copiously detailed critique written in the form of a letter to Glanvill, More vituperated: "But what will this profane Shuffler stick to do in a dear regard to his beloved Hags, of whom he is a sworn Advocate and resolved Patron, right or wrong?" (Glanvill 1689, p. 29). Indeed, writes More, Webster will go so far as to claim that "there are no Names in all the Old Testament that signifie such a Witch that destroys Men or Beasts, that makes a visible compact with the Devil, or on whose body he fucketh . . . [even] that there is no such Witch as with whom the Devil has any thing more to do than with any other sinner. . . . Take notice how weak and childish, or wild and impudent, Mr. Webster has been . . . in the behalf of his Sage Dames" (p.39). In conclusion, More laments: "That this Gallant of Witches [attempts] to secure his old Wives from being so much as in a capacity of ever being suspected for Witches, is a thing extremely coarse, and intolerably sordid" (p. 46).

In fact, Webster's polemic had been motivated more by theological and philosophical concerns than by solicitude for the women who had been branded as witches. His principal argument, derived from Paracelsus, was that natural magic was fully sufficient to account for nature's phenomena, material or immaterial. In the alchemical vision, all experience was interpreted as a manifestation of God; there was no need to invoke the Devil. But, as Thomas Jobe argues (1981, pp. 343–55), in the philosophical scheme of Glanvill and More, there was such a need. For them, the merging of spirit and matter underlying the alchemical vision represented both philosophical and religious dangers; on the other hand, too radical a split between the two threatened to lead to atheism. Spirit and matter must be neither disjoint nor interpenetrating. Some mediation was necessary to preserve the balance. And demonology furnished the answer they needed: it provided a defense against the alchemists on one side and against the feared atheism of the Cartesians on the other.[14] For these men, nature was not yet a machine (see n. 11). In the mid-seventeenth century it was evident to perhaps most natural philosophers that spirits do manifest themselves in nature (see Thomas, 1971, especially pp. 578–79); but to More and Glanvill, these spirits were necessarily the spirits of evil demons. They invoked the Devil much as Newton would soon invoke gravitational force to mediate between the Divine and the material. They could accept the reality of such occult feats of nature as the Paracelsians claimed but only as "Fathered upon the Devil" (More 1712, pp. 168–69). Given that these phenomena represented material manifestations of demonic spirits, they argued (see Glanvill above, p. 56) that the empirical method was just as appropriate for their study as for the study of ordinary phenomena.

But such investigations must proceed cautiously, they warned, and not in the manner advocated by the alchemists. Glanvill warned that true and pious scientists must not be tempted to pursue the "recondite knowledge" that belongs to Satan, but must "take care to keep themselves within the Bounds of sober Enquiry, and not indulge irregular Sollicitudes about the knowledge of Things, which Providence hath thought fit to conceal from us" (Glanvill, in Jobe 1981, p. 350). The issue for Glanvill was not simply truth versus falsity, but proper versus improper knowledge. So it was also for More, who saw the alchemists' penchant for "tumbling off, and trying tricks with *Matter*" as clearly exceeding philosophical propriety. In allowing a kinship between knowledge and erotic sexuality, and between experimental and spiritual knowledge, alchemical science not only failed to demarcate Nature adequately: it failed to

14. Keith Thomas (1971, p. 591) quotes the Cambridge Platonist Ralph Cudworth as an example: "If there be once any visible ghosts or spirits acknowledged as things permanent, it will not be easy for any to give a reason why there might not be one supreme ghost also, presiding over them all and the whole world."

demarcate the "Bounds of sober Enquiry"—the domain of proper knowledge. Its understandings remained subverted by the "Woman in us," seducing us into the "recondite knowledge," which is, by its nature, ungodly, even Satanic.

Witchcraft and Sexuality

From the usual modern standpoint, the association of these early proponents of rational science with the belief in witchcraft, and hence with the persecution of witches, appears anomalous if not somewhat embarrassing. I want to suggest, however, that, from another perspective, this association might be not anomalous or historically fortuitous but consistent and even historically appropriate. At first glance, it indicates that rationality, by present day criteria, was not entirely on the side of the early modern scientists. But what is in question here is the particular character of their ideological commitments—especially the relevance of the commitment, voiced by so many of the early Fellows of the Royal Society, to an unambiguously "masculine" science. To More and Glanvill at least, the alchemists appeared threatening not only because of their religious and political radicalism, as others have argued, but also because of their commitment to a science steeped in erotic sexual imagery and, simultaneously, to the symbolic equality of women before God. Theirs was clearly not a "masculine" science.

To the alchemists, God was immanent in the material world, in woman, and in sexuality. To More and Glanvill, chastity was a condition for Godliness; and truth, rather than being "hid in every body" (Hill 1975, p. 293), was the province of the dispassionate intellect. In their view, much of what the alchemists took to be the sign of God was in truth the mark of the Devil. The emphasis the alchemists placed on the powers of love and on the kinship between sexual intercourse and knowledge threatened to embroil the new science simultaneously in passion and heresy; it endangered science's emerging claims to purity. The witch, taken seriously as having effective powers, provided a natural focus for anxiety. What was philosophically and theologically disreputable in the alchemist was directly culpable in the witch. From the perspective of seventeenth-century cosmology, she represented precisely the invitation of Satan that is born of unbridled sexuality.

In 1486 the *Malleus Maleficarum* (Kramer and Sprenger) had proclaimed: "All witchcraft comes from carnal lust, which is in women insatiable. . . . Wherefore for the sake of their lusts [women] consort with devils." Two centuries later, at the moment in which modern science was being born, witches still embodied the fearful dangers of female sexual power. It is here that one finds the key to the logical consistency of a position in which men whom we have counted among the "mechanical philosophers" are moved to invoke the fear of witchcraft in their dispute with the alchemists.

In seventeenth-century England, the witch mania reached its apogee, and so, it might be argued, did the fear of female sexuality. In the drama of the period we see contemporary social and economic upheavals mirrored by a particularly acute preoccupation with gender and sexuality. *The White Devil, The Changling,* and even *Antony and Cleopatra* all link female sexual excess with social disorder and disintegration. The soldier in Walter Charleton's *Ephesian Matron,* published in 1659, echoes against woman in general the natural philsopher's diatribe against witches:

> You are the true *Hiena's,* that allure us with the fairness of your skins; and when folly hath brought us within your reach, you leap upon us and devour us. You are the traitors to Wisdom: the impediment to Industry . . . the clogs to virtue, and goads that drive us to all Vice, Impiety and ruine. You are the Fools Paradise, the Wisemans Plague, and the grand Error of Nature. (quoted in Easlea 1980, p. 242)

This is a character speech, not a philosopher's stand; nevertheless it presumes some resonance in its audience: a mind-set that can see all women as potential witches.

The arguments of More and Glanvill were faithful both to the anxieties of their time and to their own aspirations for the future. The reality of witchcraft effectively attested to the gravity of the dangers represented by women—dangers against which reason and the new science promised protection. It reinforced the arguments for banishing Woman, sexuality, and the correlative "unsober" inquiry of the alchemists from science. The new mechanical vision provided a secure intellectual domain for masculinity by excluding even allegorical cooperation between male and female—both in its picture of the scientist and in its picture of nature. By promising power and domination, it provided an efficacious antidote to the threats men had come to conflate with women and sexuality. Belief in witches, in turn, made this vision seem more rather than less compelling. In the ideological system that emerged and prevailed, science was a purely male and chaste venture, seeking dominion over, rather than commingling with, a female nature; it promised, and indeed helped promote, the simultaneous vanquishing of nature and of female voracity.[15]

Shifting Ideologies of Gender

The seventeenth century was a time of dramatic social, economic, and political (as well as intellectual) upheaval. The nexus among ideologies of woman, nature, and science, I argue, is essential to an understanding of the relations between the scientific and sociopolitical developments of the time. The shift in perceptions of woman and nature that I associate with the institutionalization of modern science must be understood as taking place against a background of many other transformations occurring in the culture at large,[16] and especially of the ideology of gender.

Throughout Europe, prevailing concepts of gender had been subtly shifting for over 200 years, and by the end of the seventeenth century the multiplicity of male and female roles that had previously been acceptable was considerably reduced. Definitions of *male* and *female* were becoming polarized in ways that were eminently well suited to the growing division between work and home required by early industrial capitalism. A new kind of wedge was being driven between the spheres of women and men; over time, it resulted in a

15. In attempting to explain the decline of magic in the late seventeenth and early eighteenth centuries, Keith Thomas (1971) comments that "the period saw the emergence of a new faith in the potentialities of human initiative" and a general increase in "human self-confidence" (pp. 661, 650). My argument is that what this period saw, above all, was a new faith in male initiative and an increase in male self-confidence, and that the vision of the new science that prevailed played a key role in this increase in male self-confidence.

16. The emergence of Protestantism is, of course, a crucial dimension of these transformations—a dimension almost entirely absent from my analysis, and in pressing need of incorporation.

severe curtailment of the economic, political, and social options available to women of all classes, and especially to women of the middle and upper classes (see Kelly 1981; Davis, 1975, 1977). Central to the separation of spheres was the construction of a new ideal of womanhood, although it took another 150 years for this new ideology to come to full flower. By the nineteenth century the fearful devourer, with her insatiable lust, had given way to the "angel in the house"—a chaste, desexualized, and harmless dependent whose only function was to uphold the values of the new age. With the domestication of female power, sentimental regard and protective solicitude could safely displace the overt misogyny of earlier times.

The seventeenth century has been identified by a number of authors as an especially critical transition point in this larger transformation. In the early part of the century, concern over the bounds of propriety for male and female behavior prompted James I to seek to legislate new constraints on behavior. In 1620 he ordered the bishop of London to instruct all clergy "to inveigh vehemently against the insolencies of our women, and their wearing of broad rimmed hats, pointed doublets, their hair cut short or shorne" (Kelly 1982, p. 34). Contemporary literature, ballads, sermons, and pamphlets picked up the refrain, warning women to desist from the offending modes, now designated as masculine, and expressing mounting mistrust of female "insolencies" and anxiety about gender crossing—about women who were "masculine in their gender," and men who were feminine in their behavior (Baines 1978).

The civil war in many ways seemed to confirm those fears: political upheaval brought with it an advocacy of sexual freedom and universal education for both sexes (Hill 1975, pp. 301, 306–23). Women were a vocal and visible presence in the emergent radical sects—even as prophetesses, speaking the voice of God (Thomas 1958; Mack 1982). "The soul," wrote Samuel Torshell in 1645, "knows no difference of sex." But the radical promise of the Civil War period—with its questioning of hierarchies, of the relation of king to state, and in parallel, of husband to wife—was soon squelched. Earlier arguments for divine right regained prestige; scattered conservative attitudes cohered once more into structured belief systems. After the Restoration, gender distinctions came to be drawn more sharply than ever before: male and female were separated by ascribed *nature* and by function, with women reduced to new forms of dependency and the positions of men bolstered by new sources of authority.

Alice Clark (1919) and Sheila Rowbotham (1974) have documented the changes during this period in the economic role of women, and Ruth Perry writes: "By the late seventeenth century women's economic function had gradually shrunk to that of a *housewife*, although there had been more variety in the original occupational use of the word *wife*: fishwife, alewife, applewife, oysterwife, and so on. By the end of the eighteenth century this financial dependence seems to have been accepted as a natural state" (1980, p. 37). But perhaps most crucial were the changes in assumptions about the nature of female behavior: the roles that women could appropriately play in their public and private lives; the clothing they could wear; the degree of authority they could assume; the ways and extent to which their sexuality was perceived as threatening the prevailing order.

Little is known about the concurrent changes in the perception of female sexuality, but this much is clear. In the seventeenth century, the sexual appetites of women were widely viewed as large and problematic. By the early eighteenth century, revised sexual ideology deprived the virginal daughters of the respectable middle class of passion and desire. Sexual response was acknowledged in women after marriage, but restricted to their husbands (Thomas 1959). Finally, in the Victorian period, the growing emphasis on female chastity, and the strengthening of the double standard by the growth of the capitalistic middle class, yielded the familiar if grotesque union between an idealized, sexually desensitized angel and a lustful patriarch who transacts his sexual affairs in the subterranean spaces of the urban centers (see, for example, Marcus 1977, and now also Gay 1984).

The scientific revolution did not, of course, either initiate or effect this transformation. I suggest, however, that it did both respond to and provide crucial support for the polarization of gender required by industrial capitalism. In sympathy with, and even in response to, the growing division between male and female, public and private, work and home, modern science opted for an ever greater polarization of mind and nature, reason and feeling, objective and subjective; in parallel with the gradual desexualization of women, it offered a deanimated, desanctified, and increasingly mechanized conception of nature. In so doing, science itself became an active agent of change. The ideology of modern science gave (at least some) men a new basis for masculine self-esteem and male prowess.[17] If concepts of rationality and objectivity, and the will to dominate nature, supported the growth of a particular vision of science, they supported at the same time the institutionalization of a new definition of manhood. Given the success of modern science, defined in opposition to everything female, fears of both Nature and Woman could subside. With the one reduced to its mechanical substrate, and the other to her asexual virtue, the essence of *Mater* could be both tamed and conquered; male potency was confirmed.

Implications for Science

The subsequent history of science provides abundant evidence that the values articulated by early modern scientists were in fact effective in promoting those kinds of knowledge that would lead to the mastery, control, and domination of nature. If these are the goals that define success in science, we might generally agree that different values—such as those expressed in hermetic philosophy—could not have been as conducive to success. What is much more difficult (if not impossible) to assess is how successful different values might have been in achieving other goals, more consonant with those values, and what those goals would have been. These questions begin to sound suspiciously like the patently impossible question: What would a different science look like? Because science as we know it developed only once in history, the notion of a "different" science is to a considerable degree a contradiction in terms. Nevertheless, the history of science also shows us that science, in practice, is not and has never been a monolithic enterprise. Just as we know from recent historical scholarship that the seventeenth-century victory of mechanical over hermetic philosophy was not complete, we also know that the values embodied in the ideology that subsequently prevailed

---

17. Brian Easlea (1980) makes a similar point, arguing that modern science provided not so much a new definition of male prowess as a more effective one. He writes; "For since scientific power over natural processes, unlike magical oral power, not only 'works' but is highly efficacious, the scientists, technologists and managers of capitalist society have at their disposal a *real* means of displaying their virility and of reassuring themselves of their 'superior' masculinity" (p. 255).

have never been universally embraced by the community of working scientists. This thematic pluralism presents the historian of science with a special opportunity. Although it may be idle to ask what science would have looked like had it developed in conjunction with a different gender ideology or, even better, independent of any gender ideology, we *can* begin to examine the ways in which a commitment to a particular ideology has influenced the course of scientific development. We can do this, I suggest, by attending to the language employed in the debates that continued long after Renaissance alchemy ceased to be a viable contender—debates pertaining not only to the values and goals of science but to substantive issues of method and theory as well. It is through the analysis of such debates that we can begin to understand the selection pressures exerted by ideology in general—and gender ideology in particular—on the competition between different visions of science. These pressures are part of the process that transforms a complex pluralistic tradition into a monolithic rhetoric, overlaying, obscuring, and often distorting a wide diversity of practice.

PART TWO

The Inner World of Subjects and Objects

By contrast with modern science, the history of natural philosophy before the modern era has often been described as a history of projection. From primitive magic through astrology and alchemy, early attempts to account for natural phenomena have been indicted for their failure of objectivity: for the imposition of human hopes, desires, and fears onto the natural world. Carl Jung, for example, has argued that the medieval alchemist

> experienced his projection as a property of matter; but what he was in reality experiencing was his own unconscious. In this way he recapitulated the whole history of man's knowledge of nature. As we all know, science began with the stars, and mankind discovered in them the dominants of the unconscious. . . . : a complete projected theory of human character. Astrology is a primordial experience similar to alchemy. Such projections repeat themselves whenever man tries to explore an empty darkness and involuntarily fills it with living form. (Jung 1980, p. 245)

With the modern era, these descriptions suggest, a new form of perception came into being: a self-detachment that enabled men[1] to conceive of an autonomous universe, "operating without intention or purpose or destiny in a purely mechanical or causal way" (Elias 1978, p. 256). Indeed, it is often argued that the very success of modern science and technology rests on a new methodology that protects its inquiries from the idiosyncratic sway of human motivation. No longer filling the void with living form, man learned instead

---

1. I use the masculine generic here intentionally, for the simple reason that modern science was in fact developed not by humankind but by men.

to fill it with dead form. Nature, deanimated and mechanized, could now be put to the uses of men.

There is little question that the vision (or ideology) of science to which this description speaks has continued to provide a powerful impetus to a practice of science that has proved remarkably fruitful. But it is a thesis of this book that the ideology of modern science, along with its undeniable success, carries within it its own form of projection: the projection of disinterest, of autonomy, of alienation. My argument is not simply that the dream of a completely objective science is in principle unrealizable, but that it contains precisely what it rejects: the vivid traces of a reflected self image. The objectivist illusion reflects back an image of self as autonomous and objectified: an image of individuals unto themselves, severed from the outside world of other objects (animate as well as inanimate) and simultaneously from their own subjectivity. It is the investment in impersonality, the claim to have escaped the influence of desires, wishes, and beliefs—perhaps even more than the sense of actual accomplishment—that constitutes the special arrogance, even bravura, of modern man, and at the same time reveals his peculiar subjectivity.

The essays in this section are devoted to an examination of that subjectivity. More precisely, they are devoted to an exploration of the internal dynamics that foster the development of the particular concepts of self and other, subject and object, and masculine and feminine that are characteristic of our time. All three pairs of concepts develop in interaction with one another, in a context of cultural ideals shared by the society at large. And, of course, the internalization of social norms is mediated, first and most critically, by the family.

But these essays are not concerned with the development either of contemporary social norms or of the "modern family." They are, instead, concerned with the psychodynamics of cognitive, emotional, and sexual development within the given context of those social values and norms of family arrangements that our culture endorses; their focus is psychological rather than historical. It is taken for granted that other social and familial norms would foster a somewhat different course of psychodynamic development, and hence a different subjectivity. My ultimate question is how such differences would affect our conception of science. The connections between our subjectivity and our science are subtle and complex, but a central part of my argument is that they are crucially mediated (and maintained) by the ideology that denies their existence. Accordingly, the articulation of these connections itself effectively loosens the hold of that ideology—in turn enabling us to glimpse what a science less constrained by such an ideology might look like.

The first of these essays, "Gender and Science" (chap. 4), was originally published in 1978. It represents my earliest attempt to explore the emotional substructure underlying the conjunction of science with masculinity; indeed, it can be read as a miniature version of the book on gender and science I would have written at that time. Since then, the response of many readers has made me aware of the ways in which this essay unwittingly permits a reading of gender as a "natural" category, and I have become far more conscious (in ways that are reflected in the second and third essays) of the need to emphasize the ideological dimensions of gender.

The initial task set by "Gender and Science" is to understand the culturally pervasive association between objectivity and masculinity. I show how that association reflects and contributes to a complex network of cognitive, emotional, and sexual development. Objectivity, I argue, is the cognitive counterpart of psychological autonomy, and accordingly must be understood as rooted in interpersonal space; the capacity for objectivity develops together with the articulation of self and of gender. The essay concludes with an analysis of the ways in which objectivity remains stamped by the interpersonal drama through which it was learned. Given the polarization of masculine and feminine, objectivity, properly speaking a human goal, becomes construed as objectivism, a masculine goal, whereas subjectivity becomes construed as subjectivism, a feminine prerogative.

Chapters 5 and 6 are new. They take up the central question left unanswered in the first essay, namely, the relations among objectivity, power, and domination. Just as objectivity is to be understood as an interpersonal acquisition, here it is argued that domination, even of nonhuman others, is an interpersonal project. To see how the twin goals of science—knowledge and power—are translated into objectification and domination, we need to examine the psychodynamic roots that link these goals together. The key psychological construct is autonomy, as it was in the first essay. I explore the vicissitudes of psychic autonomy with the specific aim of understanding how an atomistic, static conception of autonomy exacerbates the need for control and the desire for domination, first, of human others, and second, of abstract or nonhuman others.

In all three essays, my argument is psychoanalytic. Along with Nancy Chodorow, Dorothy Dinnerstein, Jessica Benjamin, Jane Flax, and others, I rely especially on the branch of psychoanalytic theory, directly concerned with the development of self in relation to others, called object relations theory. In seeking to account for personality development in terms of both innate drives and actual relations with others, object relations theory permits us to understand the ways in which our earliest experiences—experiences in large part determined by socially structured family relationships—help to shape our conception of the world and our characteristic orientations to it.

But the unhappy naming of this school of psychoanalytic thought requires comment. As feminists have repeatedly pointed out, classical psychoanalytic theory is hardly exempt from the androcentric biases that permeate so much of our intellectual history, and although object relations theory has been seen as more compatible with feminism, it has not escaped these biases either. The failure to fully incorporate the experience of women—even to adequately perceive women—is especially damaging to a theory of psychological development. The very choice of the name *object relations* for a theory concerned with the development of self–other relations, particularly in the context of the mother–child relation, itself reflects the specific failure that this theory attempts to analyze: the failure to perceive the mother as subject. This fundamental flaw reverberates in the theory's preoccupation with autonomy as a developmental goal and its corresponding neglect of connectedness to others.[2] It underlies the tacit implication, common to all psychoanalytic theory, that autonomy can be bought only at the price of unrelatedness. Clearly, the use of such a theoretical framework for a feminist anal-

2. This point has been particularly emphasized, both publicly and privately, by Carol Gilligan.

ysis requires a reformulation of basic terms and concepts: "objects" need to be redefined as other subjects, and autonomy needs to be reconceived as a dynamic condition enhanced rather than threatened by connectedness to others.[3] Indeed, chapter 5, "Dynamic Autonomy: Objects as Subjects," departs from the first on precisely this point. It begins with reexamination of the development of autonomy, focusing on a dynamic interplay between self and other that fosters an ideal of autonomy crucially different from more familiar ideals. Chapter 6, "Dynamic Objectivity: Love, Power, and Knowledge," argues that this reconception of autonomy facilitates a parallel reconception of objectivity as a goal that profits from the use of subjective experience. The shift that I advocate in the norms of developmental psychology has direct application to both the ideology and practice of science. Support for this claim is offered in the case studies that comprise the third section of this book.

My use of psychoanalytic theory is premised on the belief that, even with its deficiencies, it has the potentiality for self-correction. The mode of analysis it provides is sufficiently penetrating to enable us to examine developmental failures not only in the human psyche but in the theory itself. My own use of psychoanalytic theory is accordingly undertaken with the understanding that all its terms are subject to revision as we proceed. Some of these revisions (for example, in the meaning of autonomy) are either implicitly or explicitly incorporated into the interpretation of object relations theory that I present; others are only indicated as requiring attention. All of them—and further revisions too—await the contributions and critical attention of the many other scholars thinking about the same issues.

I am well aware that not everyone will share my confidence in the value of psychoanalytic theory as a tool, or in the possibility of reworking its categories from within. Of these prima facie skeptics, as of any reader, I ask only that they consider whether in fact the approach I take sheds light on the questions I raise.

---

3. The work of Nancy Chodorow, Carol Gilligan, and Jean Baker Miller is of particular importance here. All three authors have made important contributions in their own writings to the reformulations and reconceptions that are needed.

CHAPTER FOUR

Gender and Science

> The requirements of . . . correctness in practical judgments and objectivity in theoretical knowledge . . . belong as it were in their form and their claims to humanity in general, but in their actual historical configuration they are masculine throughout. Supposing that we describe these things, viewed as absolute ideas, by the single word "objective," we then find that in the history of our race the equation objective = masculine is a valid one.
>
> SIMMEL, quoted by Horney (1926, p. 200)

In articulating the commonplace, Simmel steps outside the convention of academic discourse. The historically pervasive association between masculine and objective, more specifically between masculine and scientific, is a topic that academic critics resist taking seriously. Why is that? Is it not odd that an association so familiar and so deeply entrenched is a topic only for informal discourse, literary allusion, and popular criticism? How is it that formal criticism in the philosophy and sociology of science has failed to see here a topic requiring analysis? The virtual silence of at least the nonfeminist academic community on this subject suggests that the association of masculinity with scientific thought has the status of a myth which either cannot or should not be examined seriously. It has simultaneously the air of being "self-evident" and "nonsensical"— the former by virtue of existing in the realm of common knowledge (that is, everyone knows it), and the latter by virtue of lying outside

Adapted by permission of the publishers from "Gender and Science," *Psychoanalysis and Contemporary Thought* 1 (3), 1978, pp. 409–33.

the realm of formal knowledge, indeed conflicting with our image of science as emotionally and sexually neutral. Taken seriously, it would suggest that, were more women to engage in science, a different science might emerge. Such an idea, although sometimes expressed by nonscientists, clashes openly with the formal view of science as being uniquely determined by its own logical and empirical methodology.

The survival of mythlike beliefs in our thinking about science, the very archetype of antimyth, ought, it would seem, to invite our curiosity and demand investigation. Unexamined myths, wherever they survive, have a subterranean potency; they affect our thinking in ways we are not aware of, and to the extent that we lack awareness, our capacity to resist their influence is undermined. The presence of the mythical in science seems particularly inappropriate. What is it doing there? From where does it come? And how does it influence our conceptions of science, of objectivity, or, for that matter, of gender?

These are the questions I wish to address, but before doing so it is necessary to clarify and elaborate the system of beliefs in which science acquires a gender—a system that amounts to a "genderization" of science. Let me make clear at the outset that the issue that requires discussion is *not*, or at least not simply, the relative absence of women in science. Although it is true that most scientists have been, and continue to be, men, the makeup of the scientific population hardly accounts, by itself, for the attribution of masculinity to science as an intellectual domain. Most culturally validated intellectual and creative endeavors have, after all, historically been the domain of men. Few of these endeavors, however, bear so unmistakably the connotation of masculine in the very nature of the activity. To both scientists and their public, scientific thought is male thought, in ways that painting and writing—also performed largely by men—have never been. As Simmel observed, objectivity itself is an ideal that has a long history of identification with masculinity. The fact that the scientific population is, even now, a population that is overwhelmingly male, is itself a consequence rather than a cause of the attribution of masculinity to scientific thought.[1] What requires

1. For a further elaboration of this theme, see "Women in Science: A Social Analysis" (Keller 1974).

discussion is a *belief* rather than a reality, although the ways in which reality is shaped by our beliefs are manifold and also need articulating.

How does this belief manifest itself? It used to be commonplace to hear scientists, teachers, and parents assert quite baldly that women cannot, should not, be scientists, that they lack the strength, rigor, and clarity of mind for an occupation that properly belongs to men. Now that the women's movement has made such naked assertions offensive, open acknowledgment of the continuing belief in the intrinsic masculinity of scientific thought has become less fashionable. It continues, however, to find daily expression in the language and metaphors we use to describe science. When we dub the objective sciences "hard" as opposed to the softer (that is, more subjective) branches of knowledge, we implicitly invoke a sexual metaphor, in which "hard" is of course masculine and "soft" feminine. Quite generally, facts are "hard," feelings "soft." "Feminization" has become synonymous with sentimentalization. A woman thinking scientifically or objectively is thinking "like a man"; conversely, a man pursuing a nonrational, nonscientific argument is arguing "like a woman."

The linguistic rooting of this stereotype is not lost among children, who remain perhaps the most outspoken and least self-conscious about its expression. From strikingly early ages, even in the presence of astereotypic role models, children learn to identify mathematics and science as male. "Science," my five-year-old son declared, confidently bypassing the fact that his mother was a scientist, "is for men!" The identification between scientific thought and masculinity is so deeply embedded in the culture at large that children have little difficulty internalizing it. They grow up not only expecting scientists to be men but also perceiving scientists as more "masculine" than other male professionals—for example, those in the arts. Numerous studies of masculinity and femininity in the professions confirm this observation, with the "harder" sciences as well as the "harder" branches of any profession consistently characterized as more masculine.

In one particularly interesting study of attitudes prevalent among English schoolboys, a somewhat different but critically related dimension of the cultural stereotype emerges. Hudson (1972) observes that scientists are perceived as not only more masculine than artists but simultaneously as less sexual. He writes:

> The arts are associated with sexual pleasure, the sciences with sexual restraint. The arts man is seen as having a good-looking, well-dressed wife with whom he enjoys a warm sexual relation; the scientist as having a wife who is dowdy and dull, and in whom he has no physical interest. Yet the scientist is seen as masculine, the arts specialist as slightly feminine. (p. 83)

In this passage we see the genderization of science linked with another, also widely perceived, image of science as antithetical to Eros. These images are not unrelated, and it is important to bear their juxtaposition in mind as we attempt to understand their sources and functions. What is at issue here is the kind of images and metaphors with which science is surrounded. If we can take the use of metaphor seriously, while managing to keep clearly in mind that it is metaphor and language which are being discussed, then we can attempt to understand the influences they might exert—how the use of language and metaphor can become hardened into a kind of reality.

Much attention has been given recently to the technological abuses of modern science, and in many of these discussions blame is directed toward the distortions of the scientific program intrinsic in its ambition to dominate nature without, however, offering an adequate explanation of how that ambition comes to be intrinsic to science. Generally such distortions are attributed to technology, or applied science, which is presumed to be clearly distinguishable from pure science. In the latter the ambition is supposed to be pure knowledge, uncontaminated by fantasies of control. Although it is probably true that the domination of nature is a more central feature of technology, it is impossible to draw a clear line between pure and applied science. History reveals a most complex relation between the two, as complex perhaps as the interrelation between the dual constitutive motives for knowledge: transcendence and power. It would be naive to suppose that the connotations of masculinity and conquest affect only the uses to which science is put and leave its structure untouched.

Science bears the imprint of its genderization not only in the ways it is used but in the description of reality it offers—even in the relation of the scientist to that description. To see this, it is necessary to examine more fully the implications of attributing masculinity to the very nature of scientific thought.

Having divided the world into two parts—the knower (mind) and the knowable (nature)—scientific ideology goes on to prescribe a very specific relation between the two. It prescribes the interactions which can consummate this union, that is, which can lead to knowledge. Not only are mind and nature assigned gender, but in characterizing scientific and objective thought as masculine, the very activity by which the knower can acquire knowledge is also genderized. The relation specified between knower and known is one of distance and separation. It is that between a subject and an object radically divided, which is to say, no worldly relation. Simply put, nature is objectified. Bacon's "chaste and lawful marriage" is consummated through reason rather than feeling, through "observation" rather than "immediate" sensory experience. The modes of intercourse are defined so as to ensure emotional and physical inviolability for the subject. Concurrent with the division of the world into subject and object is, accordingly, a division of the forms of knowledge into "subjective" and "objective." The scientific mind is set apart from what is to be known, that is, from nature, and its autonomy—and hence the reciprocal autonomy of the object—is guaranteed (or so it had traditionally been assumed) by setting apart its modes of knowing from those in which that dichotomy is threatened. In this process, the characterization of both the scientific mind and its modes of access to knowledge as masculine is indeed significant. Masculine here connotes, as it so often does, autonomy, separation, and distance. It connotes a radical rejection of any commingling of subject and object, which are, it now appears, quite consistently identified as male and female.

What is the real significance of this system of beliefs, whose structure now reveals an intricate admixture of metaphysics, cognitive style, and sexual metaphor? If we reject the position, as I believe we must, that the associations between scientific and masculine are simply "true"—that they reflect a biological difference between male and female brains—then how are we to account for our adherence to them? Whatever intellectual or personality characteristics may be affected by sexual hormones, it has become abundantly clear that our ideas about the differences between the sexes far exceed what can be traced to mere biology; that, once formed, these ideas take on a life of their own—a life sustained by powerful cultural and psychological forces. Even the brief discussion offered above makes it evident that, in attributing gender to an intellectual posture, in sexualizing a thought process, we inevitably invoke the large world of affect. The task of explaining the associations between masculine and scientific thus becomes, short of reverting to an untenable biological reductionism, the task of understanding the emotional substructure that links our experience of gender with our cognitive experience.

The nature of the problem suggests that, in seeking an explanation of the origins and endurance of this mythology, we look to the processes by which the capacity for scientific thought develops, and the ways in which those processes are intertwined with emotional and sexual development. Doing this makes it possible to acquire deeper insight into the structure and perhaps even the functions of the mythology we seek to elucidate. The route I wish to take proceeds along ground laid by psychoanalysts and cognitive psychologists, along a course shaped by the particular questions I have posed. What emerges is a scenario supported by the insights these workers have attained, and held together, it is to be hoped, by its own logical and intuitive coherence.

The Development of Objectivity

The crucial insight that underlies much of this discussion—an insight for which we are indebted to both Freud and Piaget—is that the capacity for objectivity, for delineating subject from object, is *not* inborn, although the potential for it no doubt is. Rather, the ability to perceive reality "objectively" is acquired as an inextricable part of the long and painful process by which the child's sense of self is formed. In the deepest sense, it is a function of the child's capacity for distinguishing self from not-self, "me" from "not-me." The consolidation of this capacity is perhaps the major achievement of childhood development.

After half a century's clinical observations of children and adults the developmental picture that has emerged is as follows. In the early world of the infant, experiences of thoughts, feelings, events, images, and perceptions are continuous. Boundaries have not yet been drawn to distinguish the child's internal from external environment; nor has order or structure been imposed on either.[2] The external environment, for most children consisting primarily of the mother during this early period, is experienced as an extension of the child. It is only through the assimilation of cumulative experiences of pleasure and pain, of gratification and disappointment, that the child slowly learns to distinguish between self and other, between image and percept, between subject and object. The growing ability to distinguish his or her self from the environment allows for the recognition of an external reality to which the child can relate— at first magically, and ultimately objectively. In the course of time, the inanimate becomes released from the animate, objects from their perspective, and events from wishes; the child becomes capable of objective thought and perception. The process by which this development occurs proceeds through sequential and characteristic stages of cognitive growth, stages that have been extensively documented and described by Piaget and his co-workers.

The background of this development is fraught with intense emotional conflict. The primary object that the infant carves out of the matrix of his/her experiences is an emotional "object," namely, the mother. And along with the emergence of the mother as a separate being comes the child's painful recognition of his/her own separate existence. Anxiety is unleashed, and longing is born. The child (infant) discovers dependency and need—and a primitive form of love. Out of the demarcation between self and mother arises a longing to undo that differentiation, an urge to reestablish the original unity. At the same time, there is also growing pleasure in autonomy, which itself comes to feel threatened by the lure of an earlier state. The process of emotional delineation proceeds in fits and starts, propelled and inhibited by conflicting impulses, desires, and fears. The parallel process of cognitive delineation must be negoti-

2. Since this article was first published, new research in infant studies has produced increasing evidence challenging the sweep of these assumptions (see Stern 1983). Although this evidence does not alter the essential structure of my own argument, it will undoubtedly give rise to future modifications in our understanding of developmental dynamics beyond the modifications discussed in chaps. 4 and 5.

ated against the background of these conflicts. As objects acquire a separate identity, they remain for a long time tied to the self by a network of magical ties. The disentanglement of self from world, and of thoughts from things, requires relinquishing the magical bonds that have kept them connected. It requires giving up the belief in the omnipotence—now of the child, now of the mother—that perpetuates those bonds and learning to tolerate the limits and separateness of both. It requires enduring the loss of a wish-dominated existence in exchange for the rewards of living "in reality." In doing so, the child moves from the egocentricity of a self-dominated contiguous world to the recognition of a world outside and independent of him/herself: a world in which objects can take on a "life" of their own.

Thus far my description has followed the standard developmental account. The recognition of the independent reality of both self and other is a necessary precondition both for science and for love. It may not, however, be sufficient—for either. Certainly the capacity for love, for empathy, for artistic creativity requires more than a simple dichotomy between subject and object. Autonomy too sharply defined, reality too rigidly defined, cannot encompass the emotional and creative experiences that give life its fullest and richest depth. Autonomy must be conceived of more dynamically and reality more flexibly if they are to allow for the ebb and flow of love and play. Emotional growth does not end with the mere acceptance of one's own separateness; perhaps it is fair to say that it begins there. Out of a condition of emotional and cognitive union with the mother, the child gradually gains enough confidence in the enduring reality of both him/herself and the environment to tolerate their separateness and mutual independence. A sense of self becomes delineated, in opposition, as it were, to the mother. Ultimately, however, both sense of self and of other become sufficiently secure to permit momentary relaxation of the boundary between—without, that is, threatening the loss of either. One has acquired confidence in the enduring survival of both self and other as vitally autonomous. Out of this recognition and acceptance of one's aloneness in the world, it becomes possible to transcend one's isolation, to truly love another.[3] The final step—of reintroducing ambiguity into one's re-

3. See, e.g., Kernberg (1977) for a psychoanalytic discussion of love.

lation to the world—is a difficult one. It evokes deep anxieties and
fears stemming from old conflicts and older desire. The ground of
one's selfhood was not easily won, and experiences that appear to
threaten the loss of that ground can be seen as acutely dangerous.
Milner (1957), in seeking to understand the essence of what makes
a drawing "alive," and conversely, the inhibitions that impede artistic
expression, has written with rare perspicacity and eloquence about
the dangers and anxieties attendant upon opening ourselves to the
creative perception so critical for a successful drawing. But unless
we can, the world of art is foreclosed to us. Neither love nor art can
survive the exclusion of a dialogue between dream and reality, between inside and outside, between subject and object.

Our understanding of psychic autonomy and, along with it, of
emotional maturity, owes a great deal to the work of the English
psychoanalyst Winnicott. Of particular importance here is Winnicott's concept of the transitional object: an object intermediate between self and other (as, for example, the baby's blanket). It is called
a transitional object insofar as it facilitates the transition from the
state of magical union with the mother to autonomy, the transition
from belief in omnipotence to acceptance of the limitations of every-
day reality. Gradually, it is given up,

> not so much forgotten as relegated to limbo. By this I mean
> that in health the transitional object does not "go inside"
> nor does the feeling about it necessarily undergo repres-
> sion. . . . It loses meaning, and this is because the transi-
> tional phenomena have become diffused, have become
> spread out over the whole intermediate territory between
> "inner psychic reality" and "the external world as perceived
> by two persons in common," that is to say, over the whole
> cultural field. (Winnicott 1971, p. 5)

To the diffuse survival of the "creative apperception" he attributes
what, "more than anything else, makes the individual feel that life
is worth living" (p. 65). Creativity, love, and play are located by
Winnicott in the "potential space" between the inner psychic space
of "me" and the outer social space of "not-me"—"the neutral area
of experience which will not be challenged"—about which "we will
never ask the question: Did you conceive of this or was it presented
to you from without?" (p. 12).

The inability to tolerate such a potential space leads to psychic distress as surely as the complementary failure to delineate adequately between self and other. "These two groups of people come to us for psychotherapy because in the one case they do not want to spend their lives irrevocably out of touch with the facts of life and in the other because they feel estranged from dream" (p. 67). Both inadequate and excessive delineation between self and other can be seen as defenses, albeit opposite ones, against ongoing anxiety about autonomy.

Emotional maturity, then, implies a sense of reality that is neither cut off from, nor at the mercy of, fantasy; it requires a sufficiently secure sense of autonomy to allow for that vital element of ambiguity at the interface between subject and object. In the words of Loewald (1959), "Perhaps the so-called fully developed, the mature ego is not one that has become fixated at the presumably highest or latest stage of development, having left the others behind it, but is an ego that integrates its reality in such a way that the earlier and deeper levels of ego-reality integration remain alive as dynamic sources of higher organization" (p. 18).

Although most of us will recognize the inadequacy of a static conception of autonomy as an emotional ideal, it is easy to fall into the trap of regarding it as an appropriate ideal for cognitive development. That is, cognitive maturity is frequently identified with a posture in which objective reality is perceived and defined as radically divided from the subjective. Our inclination to accept this posture as a model for cognitive maturity is undoubtedly influenced by the definition of objectivity we have inherited from classical science—a definition rooted in the premise that the subject can and should be totally removed from our description of the object. Though that definition has proven unquestionably efficacious in the past, contemporary developments in both philosophy and physics have demonstrated its epistemological inadequacy. They have made it necessary for us to look beyond the classical dichotomy to a more dynamic conception of reality, and a more sophisticated epistemology to support it.

If scientists have exhibited a reluctance to do so, as I think they have, that reluctance should be examined in the light of what we know about the relation between cognitive and emotional development. Elsewhere (see chap. 8) I have attempted to show the persistence of demonstrably inappropriate classical ideas even in contemporary physics, from where the most dramatic evidence for the failure of classical ideas has come. There I try to establish some of the consequences of this persistence, and to account for the tenacity of such ideas. In brief, I argue that the adherence to an outmoded, dichotomous conception of objectivity might be viewed as a defense against anxiety about autonomy of exactly the same kind that we find interfering with the capacity for love and creativity. When even physics reveals "transitional phenomena"—phenomena, that is, about which it cannot be determined whether they belong to the observer or the observed—then it becomes essential to question the adequacy of traditional "realist" modes for cognitive maturity as well as for reality. Our very definition of reality requires constant refinement as we continue in the effort to wean our perceptions from our wishes, our fears, and our anxieties; insofar as our conception of cognitive maturity is dictated by our definition of reality, that conception requires corresponding refinement.

The Development of Gender

What, the reader may ask, has all this to do with gender? Although the discussion has led us on a sizable detour, the implicit argument that relates it to the genderization of science should already be clear. Before articulating the argument more explicitly, however, we need an account of the development of gender identity and gender identifications in the context of the developmental picture I have presented thus far.

Perhaps the single most important determinant of our conceptions of male and female is provided by our perceptions of and experiences with our parents. Although the developmental processes described above are equally relevant for children of both sexes, their implications for the two sexes are bound to differ. The basic and fundamental fact that it is, for most of us, our mothers who provide the emotional context out of which we forge the discrimination between self and other, inevitably leads to a skewing of our perceptions of gender. As long as our earliest and most compelling experiences of merging have their origin in the mother–child relation, it appears to be inevitable that that experience will tend to be identified with "mother," while delineation and separation are experienced as a negation of "mother," as "not-mother." In the extrication of self from other, the mother, beginning as the first and most primitive subject, emerges, by a process of effective and affective negation, as the first object.[4] The very processes (both cognitive and emotional) that remind us of that first bond become colored by their association with the woman who is, and forever remains, the archetypal female. Correspondingly, the processes of delineation and objectification are colored by their origins in the process of separation *from* the mother; they become marked, as it were, as "not-mother." The mother becomes an object, and the child a subject, by a process that itself becomes an expression of opposition to and negation of "mother."

Although there is an entire world that exists beyond the mother, in the family constellation with which we are most familiar it is primarily the father (or the father figure) toward whom the child turns for protection from the fear of reengulfment, from the anxieties and fears of disintegration of a still very fragile ego. It is the father who comes to stand for individuation and differentiation—for objective reality itself; who indeed can represent the "real" world by virtue of being *in* it.

For Freud, reality becomes personified by the father during the oedipal conflict; it is the father who, as the representative of external reality, harshly intrudes on the child's (that is, boy's) early romance with the mother—offering his protection and future fraternity as the reward for the child's acceptance of the "reality principle." Since Freud, however, it has become increasingly well understood that the rudiments of both gender and reality are established long before the oedipal period, and that reality becomes personified by the father as soon as the early maternal bond comes to be experienced as threatening engulfment, or loss of ego boundaries. A particularly pertinent discussion of this process is presented by Loewald (1951), who writes:

> Against the threatening possibility of remaining in or sinking back into the structureless unity from which the ego emerged, stands the powerful paternal force. . . . While the primary narcissistic identity with the mother forever con-

4. To the extent that she personifies nature, she remains, for the scientific mind, the final object as well.

stitutes the deepest unconscious origin and structural layer of ego and reality, and the motive force for the ego's "remarkable striving toward unification, synthesis"—this primary identity is also the source of the deepest dread, which promotes, in identification with the father, the ego's progressive differentiation and structuralization of reality. (pp. 15–17)

Thus it is that for all of us—male and female alike—our earliest experiences incline us to associate the affective and cognitive posture of objectification with the masculine, while all processes that involve a blurring of the boundary between subject and object tend to be associated with the feminine.

The crucial question of course is: What happens to these early associations? Although the patterns that give rise to them may be quasi-universal (though strongest, no doubt, in our own form of nuclear family), the conditions that sustain them are not. It is perhaps at this point that specific cultural forces intrude most prominently. In a culture that validates subsequent adult experiences that transcend the subject–object divide, as we find for example in art, love, and religion, these early identifications can be counteracted—provided, that is, that such experiences are validated as essentially human rather than as "feminine" experience. However, in a culture such as ours, where primary validation is accorded to a science that has been premised on a radical dichotomy between subject and object, and where all other experiences are accorded secondary, "feminine" status, the early identifications can hardly fail to persist. The genderization of science—as an enterprise, as an intellectual domain, as a world view—simultaneously reflects and perpetuates associations made in an earlier, prescientific era. If this is true, adherence to an objectivist epistemology, in which truth is measured by its distance from the subjective, has to be reexamined when it emerges that, by this definition, truth itself has become genderized.

It is important to emphasize that what I have been discussing is a system of *beliefs* about the meaning of masculine and feminine rather than any either intrinsic or actual differences between male and female. Children of both sexes learn essentially the same set of ideas about the characteristics of male and female. How they then make use of these ideas in the development of their gender identity as male or female is another question. The relation between the sexual stereotypes we believe in and our actual experience and even observation of gender is a very complex one. It is crucial, however, to make a vigilant effort to distinguish between belief and reality, even, or especially, when the reality that emerges is so influenced by our beliefs. I have not been claiming, for example, that men are by nature more objective, better suited for scientific work, or that science, even when characterized by an extreme objectivist epistemology, is intrinsically masculine. What I have been discussing are the reasons we might believe such claims to be true. These beliefs may in fact lead to observed differences between the sexes, though the question of actual differences between men and women in a given culture is ultimately an empirical one. The subsequent issue of how those possible differences might be caused by cultural expectations is yet another issue, and requires separate discussion. Without getting into the empirical question of sex differences, about which there is a great deal of debate, it seems reasonable to suggest that our early beliefs about gender are (inevitably) subject to some degree of internalization.

To return to the issue of gender development, it is important to recognize that, although children of both sexes must learn equally to distinguish self from other and have essentially the same need for autonomy, to the extent that boys rest their sexual identity on an opposition to what is both experienced and defined as feminine, the development of their gender identity is likely to accentuate the process of separation. As boys, they must undergo a twofold "disidentification from mother" (Greenson 1968): first for the establishment of a self-identity, and second for the consolidation of a male gender identity. Further impetus is added to this process by the external cultural pressure on the young boy to establish a stereotypic masculinity, now culturally as well as privately connoting independence and autonomy. The traditional cultural definitions of masculine as what can never appear feminine and of autonomy as what can never be relaxed conspire to reinforce the child's earliest associations of female with the pleasures and dangers of merging, and male with both the comfort and the loneliness of separateness. The boy's internal anxiety about both self and gender is here echoed by the cultural anxiety; together they can lead to postures of exaggerated and rigidified autonomy and masculinity that can—indeed that may be designed to—defend against the anxiety and the longing that generates it. Many psychoanalysts have come to believe that, because of the boy's need to switch his identification from the mother to the father, his sense of gender identity tends always to be more fragile than the girl's. On the other hand, her sense of self-identity may be comparatively more vulnerable. It has been suggested that the girl's development of a sense of separateness may be to some degree hampered by her ongoing identification with her mother. Although she too must disentangle her "self" from the early experience of oneness, she continues to look toward her mother as a model for her gender identity. Whatever vicissitudes her relation to her mother may suffer during subsequent development, a strong identification based on common gender is likely to persist—her need for "disidentification" is not so radical. Cultural forces may further complicate her development of autonomy by stressing dependency and subjectivity as feminine characteristics. To the extent that such traits become internalized, they can be passed on through the generations by leading to an accentuation of the symbiotic bond between mother and daughter (see, for example, Chodorow 1974, 1978).

Thus it seems appropriate to suggest that one possible outcome of these processes is that boys may be more inclined toward excessive and girls toward inadequate delineation: growing into men who have difficulty loving and women who retreat from science. What I am suggesting, and indeed trying to describe, is a network of interactions between gender development, a belief system that equates objectivity with masculinity, and a set of cultural values that simultaneously (and conjointly) elevates what is defined as scientific and what is defined as masculine. The structure of this network is such as to perpetuate and exacerbate distortions in *any* of its parts—including the acquisition of gender identity.

The Development of Scientists

Whatever differences between the sexes such a network might generate (and, as I have said earlier, the existence of such differences remains ultimately an empirical question), they are in any case certain to be overshadowed by the inevitably large variations that exist within both the male and female populations. Not all men become scientists. A science that advertises itself as revealing a reality in which subject and object are unmistakably distinct may perhaps offer special comfort to those who, as individuals (be they male or female), retain particular anxiety about the loss of autonomy. In short, if we can take the argument presented thus far seriously, then we must follow it through yet another step. Would not a characterization of science which appears to gratify particular emotional needs give rise to a self-selection of scientists—a self-selection that would, in turn, lead to a perpetuation of that same characterization? Without attempting a detailed discussion of either the appropriateness of the imagery with which science is advertised or of the personality characteristics such imagery might select for, it seems reasonable to suggest that such a selection mechanism ought inevitably to operate. The persistence of the characterization of science as masculine, as objectivist, as autonomous of psychological as well as of social and political forces, would then be encouraged, through such selection, by the kinds of emotional satisfaction it provides.

If so, the question that then arises is whether, statistically, scientists do indeed tend to be more anxious about their affective as well as cognitive autonomy than nonscientists. Although it is certainly part of the popular image of scientists that they do, the actual measurement of personality differences between scientists and nonscientists has proven to be extremely difficult; it is as difficult, and subject to as much disagreement, as the measurement of personality differences between the sexes. One obvious difficulty arises out of the term *scientist*, and the enormous heterogeneity of the scientific population. Apart from the vast differences among individuals, characteristics vary across time, nationality, discipline, and, even, with degree of eminence. The Einsteins of history fail, virtually by definition, to conform to more general patterns either of personality or of intellect. Nevertheless, certain themes, however difficult they may be to pin down, continually reemerge with enough prominence to warrant consideration. These are the themes, or stereotypes, on which I have concentrated throughout this essay, and though they can neither exhaustively nor accurately describe science or scientists as a whole—as stereotypes never can—they do acquire a degree of corroboration from the literature on the "scientific personality." It seems worth noting, therefore, several features that emerge from a number of efforts to describe the personality characteristics which tend to distinguish scientists from nonscientists.

I have already referred to the fact that scientists, particularly physical scientists, score unusually high on "masculinity" tests, meaning only that, on the average, their responses differ greatly from those of women. At the same time, studies (for example, Roe 1953, 1956) report that they tend overwhelmingly to have been loners as children, to be low in social interests and skills, indeed to avoid interpersonal contact. McClelland's subsequent studies confirm these impressions. He writes: "And it is a fact, as Anne Roe reports, that young scientists are typically not very interested in girls, date for the first time late in college, marry the first girl they date, and thereafter appear to show a rather low level of heterosexual drive" (1962, p. 321). One of McClelland's especially interesting findings was that 90 percent of a group of eminent scientists see, in the "mother–son" picture routinely given as part of the Thematic Apperception Test, "the mother and son going their separate ways" (p. 323), a relatively infrequent response to this picture in the general population. It conforms, however, with the more general observation (emerging from biographical material) of a distant relation to the mother,[5] frequently coupled with "open or covert attitudes of derogation" (Roe 1956, p. 215).

Though these remarks are admittedly sketchy and by no means constitute a review of the field, they do suggest a personality profile that seems admirably suited to an occupation seen as simultaneously masculine and asexual. The Baconian image of a "chaste and lawful marriage" becomes remarkably apt insofar as it allows the scientist both autonomy and mastery in his marriage to a bride kept at safe, "objectified" remove.[6]

---

5. These studies are, as is evident, of male scientists. It is noteworthy, however, that studies of the relatively small number of female scientists reveal a similar, perhaps even more marked, pattern of distance in relations to the mother. For most, the father proved to be the parent of primary emotional and intellectual importance (see, e.g., Plank and Plank 1954).

6. Earlier I pointed out how Bacon's marital imagery constitutes an invitation to the "domination of nature." A fuller discussion of this posture would also require consideration of the role of aggression in the development of object relations and symbolic thought processes (an aspect that has been omitted from the present discussion). It has been suggested by Winnicott that the act of severing subject from object is experienced by the child as an act of violence, and that it carries with it forever, on some level, the feeling tone of aggression. Winnicott observes that "it is the destructive drive that creates the quality of externality" (p. 93), that, in the creation and recognition of the object there is always, and inevitably, an implicit act

Conclusion

It is impossible to conclude a discussion of the genderization of science without making some brief comments on its social implications. The linking of scientific and objective with masculine brings in its wake a host of secondary consequences that, however self-evident, may nevertheless need articulating. Not only does our characterization of science thereby become colored by the biases of patriarchy and sexism, but simultaneously our evaluation of masculine and feminine becomes affected by the prestige of science. A circular process of mutual reinforcement is established in which what is called scientific receives extra validation from the cultural preference for what is called masculine, and, conversely, what is called feminine—be it a branch of knowledge, a way of thinking, or woman herself—becomes further devalued by its exclusion from the special social and intellectual value placed on science and the model science provides for all intellectual endeavors. This circularity not only operates on the level of ideology but is assisted by the ways in which the developmental processes, both for science and for the child, internalize ideological influences. For each, pressures from the other operate, in the ways I have attempted to describe, to effect biases and perpetuate caricatures.

Neither in emphasizing the self-sustaining nature of these beliefs, nor in relating them to early childhood experience do I wish to suggest that they are inevitable. On the contrary, by examining their dynamics I mean to emphasize the existence of alternative possibilities. The disengagement of our thinking about science from our notions of what is masculine could lead to a freeing of both from some of the rigidities to which they have been bound, with profound ramifications for both. Not only, for example, might science become more accessible to women, but, far more importantly, our very con-

---

of destruction. Indeed, he says, "It is the destruction of the object that places the object outside the area of the subject's omnipotent control" (p. 90). Its ultimate survival is, of course, crucial for the child's development. "In other words, because of the survival of the object, the subject may now have started to live in the world of objects, and so the subject stands to gain immeasurably; but the price has to be paid in acceptance of the ongoing destruction in unconscious fantasy relative to object-relating" (p. 90). It seems likely that the aggressive force implicit in this act of objectification must make its subsequent appearance in the relation between the scientist and his object, that is, between science and nature.

ception of "objective" could be freed from inappropriate constraints. As we begin to understand the ways in which science itself has been influenced by its unconscious mythology, we can begin to perceive the possibilities for a science not bound by such mythology.

How might such a disengagement come about? To the extent that my analysis rests on the significance of the gender of the primary parent, changing patterns of parenting could be of critical importance.[7] But other developments might be of equal importance. Changes in the ethos that sustains our beliefs about science and gender could also come about from the current pressure (in part, politically inspired) to reexamine the traditionally assumed neutrality of science, from philosophical exploration of the boundaries or limitations of scientific inquiry, and even, perhaps especially, from events within science itself. Both within and without science, the need to question old dogma has been pressing. Of particular interest among recent developments *within* science is the growing interest among physicists in a process description of reality—a move inspired by, perhaps even necessitated by, quantum mechanics. In these descriptions, object reality acquires a dynamic character, akin to the more fluid concept of autonomy emerging from psychoanalysis. Bohr himself perspicaciously provided us with a considerably happier image than Bacon's (one more apt even for the future of physics) when he chose for his coat of arms the yin-yang symbol, over which reads the inscription: *Contraria Sunt Complementa*.

Where, finally, has this analysis taken us? In attempting to explore the significance of the sexual metaphor in our thinking about science, I have offered an explanation of its origins, its functions, and some of its consequences. Necessarily, many questions remain, and it is perhaps appropriate, by way of concluding, to articulate some of them. I have not, for example, more than touched on the social and political dynamics of the genderization of science. This is

---

7. In this I am glad to be joined by Dinnerstein (1976), who contributes an extraordinarily provocative analysis of the consequences of the fact that it is, and has always been, the mother's "hand that rocks the cradle." Her analysis, though it goes much further than the sketch provided here, essentially corroborates my own in the places where they overlap. She concludes that the human malaise resulting from the present sexual arrangements can be cured only by sharing the nurturance and care of the infant equally between the mother and the father. Perhaps that is true. I would, however, argue that, at least for the particular consequences I have discussed here, other changes might be of more immediate bearing.

a crucial dimension that remains in need of further exploration. It has seemed to me, however, that central aspects of this problem belong in the psychological domain, and further, that this is the domain least accounted for in most discussions of scientific thought.

Within the particular model of affective and cognitive development I have invoked, much remains to be understood about the interconnections between cognition and affect. Although I have, throughout, assumed an intimate relation between the two, it is evident that a fuller and more detailed conception is necessary.

Finally, the speculations I offer raise numerous questions of historical and psychological fact. I have already indicated some of the relevant empirical questions on the psychology of personality that bear on my analysis. Other questions of a more historical nature ought also to be mentioned. How, for example, have conceptions of objectivity changed with time, and to what extent have these conceptions been linked with similar sexual metaphors in other, pre-scientific eras (see, for example, part 1), or, for that matter, in other, less technological cultures? Clearly, much remains to be investigated; perhaps the present essay can serve to provoke others to help pursue these questions.

CHAPTER FIVE

Dynamic Autonomy:
Objects as Subjects

Plato and Bacon may be the two most cited forebears of modern science, but between them lies a divide more urgent than time: their incommensurability is marked above all by the gulf between love and power. Whereas the Platonic knower seeks to "approach and unite" with the essential nature of things, guided in his search by pure eros, for the Baconian scientist knowledge is equated with power; he seeks dominion over things. Both visions of knowledge are supported by images of chaste sexuality, but the difference between the two images is striking. For Plato, chastity implies a demarcation between body and soul; it serves to safeguard the erotic purity of the like-to-like relationship between the mental faculty and the objects of knowledge. By contrast, Bacon's "chaste and lawful marriage"—now between a male mind and a female nature—seems to be a metaphor for power and domination, designed to safeguard the integrity of the knower.

However, to stop at the suggestion that Bacon's marital metaphor sets modern science in a patriarchal tradition and thus *naturally* implies domination is to miss an opportunity to examine the subtler dynamics of domination in both science and patriarchy. It is, for one, to miss the complex interaction between chastity and conjugality that plays such a crucial role in Bacon's vision. This marriage is chaste because it keeps sexual congress within bounds, lawful, and hence safely under control. Unlike Plato's vision of ultimate union, and unlike the "mystic marriage" of the alchemists, Bacon's vision was of a conjunction that remains forever disjunctive. The question we must ask is this: To what extent does that disjunction carry within it a *necesssary* implication of control and power? Or, in the words

95

of a contemporary feminist scholar (Eisenstein 1979), "Is objectivity a code word for male domination?" If it is, how did it come to be so? And finally, could it be otherwise?

Even though a relation between mind and nature premised on disjunction permits the use (perhaps even exploitation) of nature, it ought not, at least in principle, be incompatible with respect for the integrity of nature, nor ought such disjunction invite aggression against, or even the domination of, nature.[1] Objectivism in and of itself seems rather to imply emotional neutrality—and indeed, that is all that science claims. True, such an epistemological premise seems distinctly better geared to the achievement of competence and mastery (in the sense of control over one's own fate) than to erotic gratification; but competence does not necessarily imply control, any more than self-mastery implies mastery over another.

How is it, then, that in scientific discourse the two are so often conflated, that objectivity leads with such apparent inexorability to control and domination?[2] The answer, I suggest, is rooted in the fact that the cognitive claims of science are not themselves objective in origin but in fact grow out of an emotional substructure. The scientist is not the purely dispassionate observer he idealizes, but a sentient being for whom the very ambition for objectivity carries with it a wealth of subjective meanings: His world of objects never ceases to reflect the "object"[3] (that is, subject) world of the child he once was. In order to understand the relation between objectivity

1. There is little question that the denial of interconnectedness between subject and object serves to nullify certain kinds of moral constraint; it *allows* for kinds of violation (even rape) of the other that would be precluded by a respect for the relation between subject and object. At the same time, however, it ought logically also serve as a protection against forms of violence provoked by a relation between subject and object that is experienced as threatening to the subject.

2. Simmel (1923, p. 104) makes the argument for a reverse relation: "From time immemorial, every domination that rests on a subjective preponderance of force has made it its business to provide itself with an objective justification: in short, to transform might into right. . . . [T]here is a sense in which the psychological superiority that is secured for expressions of the male nature by the relationship of domination between men and women develops into a logical superiority. These expressions of the male nature claim normative significance on the ground that they exhibit the objective truth and rectitutde that are equally valid for everyone, male or female."

3. The use of the word *object* to denote another subject (first and foremost the mother)—a use that object relations theory inherits from Freud—suggests the difficulty, remarked on in the introduction to this section, that even object relations theorists have in recognizing mothers as subjects in their own right.

and domination we need to inquire further into the meanings of autonomy, competence, and control.

In chapter 4, written several years ago, I explored the connections among autonomy, masculinity, and objectivity that emerge from the child's developing sense of self, gender, and reality. There is a fourth concept—corresponding to the child's developing sense of agency—that now seems to me conspicuous by its absence from that discussion: the concept of power. This crucial additional element provides, through its relationship with the triad of autonomy, masculinity, and objectivity, the key to an exploration of the complex relations between objectivity and domination.

All four of these terms admit of a range of meanings. *Autonomy,* at one end of its range, connotes a radical independence from others, mapping closely onto an interpretation of *objectivity* that implies a reductive disjunction of subject from object—an interpretation I have labeled "objectivism." It is this end of the spectrum of objectivity that, I earlier argued, correlates with a conception of masculinity denying all traces of femininity. Here I will go on to argue that the same interpretation of autonomy also correlates with a conception of power as power over others, that is, with power defined as domination. Thus the linkage between objectivity and domination that feminists have discerned is not intrinsic to the aims of science, or even to the equation between knowledge and power, but rather to the particular meanings assigned to both power and objectivity. In short, it is argued that this linkage is a derivative of the particular biases that are cast by modern Western culture on all aspects of psychological (cognitive as well as emotional) development. The aim of this essay is to question those biases: to advocate a shift of developmental norms, corresponding to a shift in the meaning of all four of these terms.

It is essential to note at the outset how laden the word *autonomy,* in particular, is with the prejudices of our culture. Indeed, the tendency to confuse autonomy with separation and independence from others is itself part of what we need to explain. Throughout this discussion, I use the term to refer to the psychological sense of being able to act under one's own volition instead of under external control. This does not mean, or even suggest, that one's actions are not *influenced* by others, or that one has no need of others.

The fact is that autonomy is never an emotionally neutral experience. Insofar as it is built on the experience of competence, the sense of self as autonomous is a profound source of pleasure. But even the satisfactions of competence are not a purely individual matter. The emotional gratification generated by one's ability to act effectively is, at root, fed by one's relation to those others with whom one remains—even (or perhaps especially) in denial—affectively bound. The question we must ask therefore is this: Under what circumstances does competence promote an enhanced sense of self and of one's ability to relate to the world, and under what circumstances are competence and mastery pursued in the service of alienation, of denied connectedness, of defensive separation—as protections against fear and dread?

In chapter 4 I reviewed some of the conflicting desires and fears accompanying and affecting the young child's articulation of self, and I emphasized the connections between these emotional struggles and the child's emerging relations between self and other, subject and object. The definition of autonomy was a key variable in this analysis. If one's sense of self is understood as mediating between the world of infantile conflicts and that of adult fulfillment, the degree of rigidity with which one seeks to define one's autonomy can be seen as reflecting both the intensity of conflicts and the degree of fulfillment possible. Autonomy too rigidly and too statically conceived precludes the creative ambiguity without which neither love nor play, nor even certain kinds of knowledge, can survive. Although such an analysis is extremely helpful to our understanding of the mind-set that confuses autonomy with separation and independence from others, it does not explain why the same mind-set tends to confuse objectivity with domination.

For this we need to backtrack and reexamine the differences between the meanings of autonomy at the two ends of its spectrum. These two contrasting conceptions, one static and the other dynamic, must now be seen as different in kind as well as in degree. The distinction between them is admittedly schematic; it reduces what is in practice a complex range (or network) of psychosocial options to two poles. The virtue of such a simplification is that it enables us to see several features of the psychological landscape more clearly: It uncovers a viable and psychologically cogent alternative to the developmental goal assumed in most psychological theory; it high-

lights the proximity between prevailing norms and certain kinds of
pathology; and it underscores the function of gender in this mapping
of psychological options.

Meanings of Autonomy

To recapitulate, a dynamic conception of autonomy leaves unchallenged a "potential space" between self and other—the "neutral
area of experience" that, as Winnicott (1971) describes it, allows the
temporary suspension of boundaries between "me" and "not-me"
required for all empathic experience—experience that allows for the
creative leap between knower and known. It acknowledges the ebb
and flow between subject and object as the prerequisite for both
love and knowledge.

In my earlier account of this process, I wrote about such a
conception of autonomy as if it required a sense of self "delineated
in opposition, as it were, to the mother"—and as if the "momentary
relaxation of boundaries" was a secondary possibility, within the
context of a secure delineation of self and other. Now it seems crucial
to emphasize that dynamic autonomy is a product at least as much
of relatedness as it is of delineation; neither is prior. Dynamic autonomy reflects a sense of self (Winnicott calls it the "true self") as
both differentiated from and related to others, and a sense of others
as subjects with whom one shares enough to allow for a recognition
of their independent interests and feelings—in short for a recognition of them as other subjects. It develops not simply out of the
experience of competence, of being able to affect others and one's
environment in ways that feel satisfying, but also, and essentially,
out of the experience of continuity and reciprocity of feeling in the
relation between infant and mother (or other primary caretaker).
This ideal—for most of us only occasionally realized—enables the
very real indeterminacy in the distinction between subject and object to function as a resource rather than as a source of confusion
and threat. In particular, it permits the use of that indeterminacy
in the interests of a clearer perception (and a more mature love) of
the other in his or her own right. Accordingly, it gives rise to a sense
of agency in a world of interacting and interpersonal agents with
whom and with which one feels an essential kinship, while still

recognizing, and accepting, their independent integrity. Agency is effective to the extent that it is based on adequate (or realistic) cognizance of the differences between oneself and another. At the same time, however, acting on the world is acting on others more or less like oneself; it is more of an acting *in* than an acting *on* the world. This is not to say that such action (like action in general) is not geared to desired ends, or that it is not in fact called forth by the desire to effect change. It is only to say that the desirability of ends is determined not simply by one's own needs but by the needs of others as well.

Where such flexibility in the boundaries between self and other can survive, the distinction between self interest and altruism begins to lose its sharpness. It does not, however, disappear. Not every difference gives rise to conflict. But conflict, both intra- and inter-personal, is an inescapable aspect of all human existence. And unlike difference per se, conflict inevitably brings with it the issue of con-trol—above and beyond the kinds of control called forth by the requirements of effective agency. It provokes the need to control oneself, or another, as a response to felt danger. Self-control here is a response to internal (or internalized) threat, while control of others is a way of responding to external (or externalized) threat. The extent to which one can maintaian clarity about the difference between self and other determines one's capacity to locate the source of threat correctly and, accordingly, to avoid slipping into self-control as an attempt to control another (or vice versa). On the other hand, the maintenance of continuity between self and other provides a check against the tendency to slip from the need to control, or contain, another with whom one is embattled, to the desire to hurt or destroy. Such continuity—an ongoing reminder of the personhood of the other—can foster the search for nonviolent solutions of interpersonal conflict and inhibit or even defuse the aggressive feelings aroused.[4]

The ideal described here requires an exquisite balancing act. It presupposes that the fears of merging, of loss of boundaries, on the one hand, and the fears of loneliness and disconnection, on the other, *can* be balanced. It also presupposes the compatibility of one's con-trasting desires for intimacy and for independence. This is not an unfamiliar ideal; it can be gleaned from the writings of the major

---

4. For a particularly thoughtful exploration of this theme, see Ruddick 1983.

object relations theorists, especially Winnicott (1971), Fairbairn (1952), and Guntrip (1961), and more explicitly, from Kohut (1971, 1977)—and it is considerably more prominent in Chodorow (1978) and Gilligan (1982). But it is not a common one. A far more usual assumption in psychological literature is that the two sets of fears and desires are neither reconcilable nor of comparable weight. As Jean Baker Miller observes, "Current workers in the psychoanalytic tradition . . . tend to see the development of self as a process of separating one's self from the matrix of others, 'becoming one's own man' [Levinson 1978]. Self-development is attained as a result of a series of painful 'crises' by which the individual accomplishes a crucial sequence of separation from others."[5] Freud himself was inclined to view love and the desire for union with others as antagonistic to both individual development (1930, p. 99) and culture. In *Civilization and its Discontents* (1930) he writes, "Love opposes the interests of culture" (p. 49). Pleasure and reality, in his starkly pessimistic view of life, emerge as opposing principles. So compelling is the urge toward union that it must be subjected to lifelong resistance; so greatly does it exceed the desire for independence that autonomy—and accordingly, in this view, selfhood as well—will develop only under duress, under the coercion of necessity.

If that description were fair, a developmental ideal implying a sharply delineated boundary between self and others would indeed make psychological sense. But even so, virtually all psychological theorists would agree that the attempt to delineate absolutely between self and other represents a miscarriage of development, or at the very least "a development that has somehow gone too far" (Shapiro 1981, p. 74)—that inhibits growth and perception as well as genuine self esteem and the capacity to love another. As such, it leads to a state of alienated selfhood, of denied connectedness, of defensive separateness—to a condition which finally leads to being "out of touch with the facts of life" (Winnicott 1971, p. 67). Autonomy then takes on the familiar definition of free and unfettered self-government, of independence of others and one's environment. But independence and self government for such individuals requires constant vigilance and control, and indeed that requirement itself is an indication of the extent to which such a psychological stance reflects

5. Jean Baker Miller, unpublished manuscript; see also Miller 1976.

prevalent fears of and anxiety about "giving in" (either to internal impulses or to external pressures)—in short, ongoing anxiety about one's autonomy.

Constant vigilance and control are the telltale marks of a conception of autonomy that in fact belies its own aims. They reflect not so much confidence in one's difference from others as resistance to (even repudiation of) sameness, not so much the strength of one's own will as the resistance to another's, not so much a sense of self-esteem as uncertainty about the durability of self—finally, not so much the security of one's ego boundaries as their vulnerability. It betrays particular fears of dependency, loss of self-control, and loss of self. Control (of one's self or another) is called forth as a way of alleviating these fears. To the extent that one's psychic world is pervaded by the sense of conflict, control seems a natural and necessary response. But it is a primarily defensive response, and its effectiveness is accordingly at best short term. For this reason, David Shapiro describes this posture (an extreme form of what I have described as static autonomy) as one of "pseudo" rather than genuine autonomy. He points out, "Flexibility—not rigidity—reflects an active self-direction. Furthermore, flexibility—not rigidity—reflects a genuinely objective attitude towards the world" (1981, pp. 74–75).

Any attempt to paint the psychic landscape with so broad a brush must necessarily miss the finer distinctions among the many kinds of personalities that have in common only the aspiration toward a rigidified or pseudoautonomy and an overly demarcated definition of self. It fails to distinguish between patent failures and ostensible successes: those whose attempts at control of others reveal evident confusion between self and other, and those for whom such attempts appear to clarify and solidify that difference. Furthermore, it does not distinguish between those many individuals who, despite an inability to love, lead productive and constructive lives and those for whom acute fears of "giving in" lead to obsessive compulsionality or even paranoia. Above all, it does not distinguish between those for whom control has the meaning of regulating and containing, and those for whom it takes on the more explicitly aggressive meaning of domination and destruction. For our present purposes, it is this last distinction that requires most immediate attention.

If control seems a natural and necessary response to conflict, an attempt to preserve or foster autonomy under conditions of adversity, domination is a response to conflict in a world of definitively unequal contestants. It is one means of establishing one's place in an already established hierarchy, in a world in which the alternative to dominance is perceived as submission. The fact that this response of course also helps to create such a world is not overlooked here. The point, however, is that the shift from control to domination cannot be understood solely in terms of the struggle for autonomy, for the delineation of self from other, but rather that it arises most critically out of the psychological assimilation of autonomy with external authority—an assimilation, or fusion, that Jessica Benjamin describes as "uniquely suited to the epoch of liberal capitalism" (1982, p. 196).[6] The developmental nexus of that assimilation will be discussed in a later section, but for now it will be useful to review the phenomenology of autonomy and authority in human psychology, particularly as it illuminates the relation between control and domination. For this, Shapiro's analysis of sadism and rigid character (1981, chaps. 5 and 6) is especially useful.

Domination

The attempt to achieve control through the domination of another is a maneuver familiar to all of us, but it takes its most extreme and most crystalline form in the sadistic personality. Indeed, Erich Fromm has argued that "the passion to have absolute and unrestricted control over a living being" (1973, p. 322) is the essence of sadism. Its primary function, he suggests, is to transform the "experience of impotence into the experience of omnipotence" (p. 323). As such, it reflects a respect for power and a contempt for weakness that the sadist shares with all authoritarian personalities. Sadism is,

6. In her own attempt to understand the conjunction of differentiation and domination, Benjamin covers much of the same ground covered here. The focus of her extremely interesting essay is, however, somewhat different from mine: it is more on the internal contradictions invoked by the assimilation of autonomy with authority and less on the elaboration of the phenomenology and consequences of that assimilation.

in this sense, a particular expression of extreme contempt for weakness and vulnerability.

Essential to the self-esteem of sadistic individuals is the existence of others in relation to whom they can demonstrate their superior power. Their place in the hierarchy, their proximity to those they respect, and their distance from those they disdain are the very measure of their self-esteem. What the sadist adds to the more generally familiar equation of power and esteem is a particularly punitive attitude toward those regarded as inferiors. As Shapiro writes, "Such persons who, for certain rigid men, may include women in general and, even more, 'effeminate' men embody what the rigid individual is ashamed of, defensively repudiates, and therefore hates. He is disgusted by them, sometimes outraged by them, even obsessively so; and if he is also in a position of actual power or authority, he may be driven to punish them. . . . Such punishment . . . reflects its essential nature: to punish 'weakness' by 'discipline,' to shame inferiority and make it aware of itself by humiliation and degradation, to 'show who's boss'" (1981, pp. 106–07).

The effect of such behavior on the victim depends crucially on the victim's ultimate capacity to "identify with the aggressor." Jean Baker Miller has drawn a distinction between "temporary" and "permanent inequality" (1976, pp. 4–6) that is critical here. For sons and military recruits, such punitive behavior is likely, and even intended, to foster the re-creation of the same stance in relation to other (future) inferiors; for women and others cast in relations of permanent inequality, it is more likely to foster the development of the reciprocal stance of victim, or masochist. In both cases, such behavior is self-reproducing:[7] it perpetuates a preoccupation with superiority and inferiority, and the equation of self-esteem with position in the power hierarchy.

Sadism is of further importance for us to examine because of its intimate dependence on sexuality, a dependence born of the eroticization of power. For the sexual sadist (or masochist) aggression not only permits sexual arousal: it is the very essence of sexual excitement. The abasement of another is a source of eroticism precisely

---

7. The reproduction of aggressive behavior from one generation to another is documented in observational studies of children. See, e.g., Bellak and Antell 1974.

because it both satisfies the need to "identify with the aggressor," that is, the desire to merge and become one with the "powerful ones above" (Shapiro 1981, p. 103), and confirms one's difference from the abhorrent and fearful weak. The abandonment of another's will to one's own is simultaneously proof of the sadist's power and of his (or her) phallic integrity. It cements one's affinity with those above and demonstrates one's distance from those below. Sexuality now takes on a very particular meaning: not mutuality but mastery, not making love but "fucking," not loss of boundaries of self but affirmation of self. As Simone de Beauvoir described it, it is the expression of "the will bent on fulfilling the flesh without losing itself in it" (1970, p. 39); as Shapiro calls it, it is a "sexuality of the will" (1981, p. 129). A point emphasized by Bataille (1977) and Jessica Benjamin (1980) is the fundamentally vicarious nature of such sexuality: the flesh is fulfilled *through* and *by means of* the other's loss of self. The sexual subjugation of the other becomes erotic by demarcating self from other in such a way as to channel contempt and fears of impotence (as well as of ego loss) away from the self to the other; at the same time, it transforms the fantasied omnipotence of the other into impotence. Impotence and dependency are now contained in the will-lessness of the other, as power is marshaled by the will of the self.[8]

The stance described here is not limited to sexual sadism. Although less distinctly, it is present in much of what we think of as normal sexuality. John Updike claims to speak for men in general when he writes, "We want to fuck what we fear" (quoted in May 1980, p. 140); the sense of control over others provided by sexual conquest may differ only in degree from that provided by rape. Shapiro concludes that "just such feelings seem to characterize the sexual attitudes of many rigid men and even a certain conception of 'manliness'" (1981, p. 133); he understates, however, the prevalence of those attitudes and that conception. Overt sadism merely exhibits in pure form a phenomenon that is pandemic in human psychology: the appetite for domination, whether sexual or nonsexual. Analysis of the psychodynamics of domination, starting from the sadistic per-

8. But, as Jessica Benjamin emphasizes in her insightful analysis of erotic domination (1980), if the will-lessness, or subjugation, of the other is to be an effective aphrodisiac, she (or he) must retain sufficient subjectivity to will her or his own violation.

sonality as extreme case, reveals that domination is a response not simply to difference or conflict, or even to inequality per se, but to inequality made threatening by the specter of difference dissolving. In short, domination is a response to the dangers of another's powerlessness evoked by one's own failure of differentiation and autonomy. Domination guarantees the indissolubility of difference by construing all difference as inequality—an inequality exacerbated by enforced vertical distance.

Autonomy and Gender

Autonomy, control, and domination lie on a continuum that does not by itself distinguish between male and female. People of both sexes struggle with the meaning of selfhood, autonomy, and intimacy, and with the need to maintain integrity of self under the stress of love, conflict, and power differentials. And in the effort to maintain that integrity of self, people of both sexes can, and do, come to look to control of self and of others as a means of bolstering their ego boundaries and, simultaneously, their self-esteem.

Nonetheless, it is a persistent fact of our culture that men tend to be especially preoccupied with questions of their autonomy and are considerably more likely than women to seek to support that autonomy through the pursuit of mastery and domination. This fact reflects not simply the greater access that men have to power but, more deeply, our very definition of what it means to be masculine. It is a reflection of the psychosocial construction of man.

The first and perhaps most critical link between autonomy and masculinity was described in the previous essay. Since that essay was written, the dynamics of gender development in the context of maternal care have been much more fully elaborated by others, especially by Nancy Chodorow (1978, 1979). What Chodorow adds to this discussion is an emphasis on the dual character of the separation–individuation process—a process leading not only to the recognition of self as different from other, but also to the ultimate recognition of the other as subject like oneself. This duality is born out of the reciprocity of the mother–child interaction. In the give and take of this interaction (abundantly documented by recent observations of mothers and infants in action), maternal recognition fosters both continuity and difference. The pleasure that the mother (or primary caretaker) reflects in the child's growing autonomy is a crucial component in the development of that autonomy. Most critically, it serves to promote a "differentiation [that] is not distinctness and separateness, but a particular way of being connected to others" (Chodorow, 1979, p. 60).

The possibility of taking pleasure in another's autonomy is itself evidence of a sense of self defined simultaneously in relation to and in differentiation from others. It presupposes an alternative to symbiosis on the one hand, and to alienation on the other. But such a sense of self, with the richly dialectical process of maternal recognition that it enables, is precisely what may be jeopardized by too much, or alternatively, by too slight an emphasis on separation and difference. In the language we have used here, the cultural definiton of male and female as polar opposites, the one premised on difference and the other on similarity, works against the development of dynamic autonomy for both sexes. It leads to a foreclosure of continuity on the one hand, and of differentiation on the other—both foreclosures equally inimical to the recognition of intersubjectivity. These sexual divisions may be quite functional in the reproduction of mothers, that is, in the creation of women who are better fitted for mothering than men (and of men more suited to the instrumental life than women). But by inhibiting the development of autonomy in women, they also serve to reproduce mothers who, because of their own underdeveloped sense of self, may feel the child's increasing autonomy as loss or rejection and may thus be unable to realize the full dyadic potential of the mothering relation. Mothers who rely on their children for the continuity on which they are socialized to depend, and which they are denied in the rest of their lives, are ill-prepared to foster the dynamic independence their children need.[9] One consequence of the polarization of gender is thus a deformation of mothering that, in turn, fosters the very conditions of its own deformation.

This calls our attention to a crucial point often lost even in feminist literature—indeed, absent from my own earlier account of psychological development: the inevitably autocatalytic and cyclical nature of the developmental process. Because mothers (as well as

9. The potential costs of this dynamic for the mother–daughter relation are insightfully elaborated in an early paper by Jane Flax (1978).

fathers) were themselves once children, any analysis of psychological development that takes the maternal (or paternal) role as a fixed point remains deficient. Psychosocial development cannot be thought of as a linear causal sequence but must instead be understood as a complexly interactive dynamic in which the constitutive factors operate as both effect and cause.

Furthermore, although an analysis that focuses primarily on the mother–child relation (especially one that acknowledges the significance of the cultural context in which development occurs) enables us to understand some of the differences between male and female children in their development of autonomy, it is not sufficient for understanding gender asymmetries in the assimilation of autonomy with power—a phenomenon that is itself a crucial ingredient in the production of parents. To explore the relations among autonomy, power, and gender, we need to amend the preceding discussion to take account of the developing child's encounter with authority, understanding as we do so that authority too is psychosocially constructed.[10] This requires further consideration of the vicissitudes of early development. Above all, it requires an examination of the central role played by the stereotypic white middle-class father in the child's consolidation of gender and autonomy.

Paternal Authority

Encounters with adult authority, particularly with intrusive parenting, can become contests of will for children of both sexes. Erikson locates the critical moment in the development of autonomy (or its failure of development) in the anal stage (see, for example, Erikson 1968), and no doubt toilet training is an arena especially susceptible to (real or imagined) interference with a child's developing autonomy. Indeed, traditional psychoanalytic theory holds the problems of this developmental stage responsible for the development of the sadistic personality. But the abuse of adult authority, and the concomitant damage to a child's growing sense of self, can occur at any time from infancy on (see, for example, Stern 1977). Such abuses can, and generally do, lead to excessive preoccupation

10. For an extensive analysis of the psychosocial and political construction of authority, see Hartsock 1983.

with control for both male and female children. Where the two sexes differ is in the markedly different ways in which such preoccupations are expressed. And these differences are determined primarily by the child's encounter with paternal authority, in short, by what is known as the oedipal resolution of preoedipal conflicts.

In traditional psychoanalytic theory, the intervention of the father in the mother–child dyad is seen as essential for differentiation. As a counter to the mother, the father's intervention is seen as especially vital for the male child. It protects him against a love that makes him "dangerously dependent on a part of the outer world, namely, on his chosen love-object" (Freud 1930, p. 47); it also protects him against the fearful power of the mother. By introducing an alternate image of power to which the male child can aspire, the father offers his son a very special kind of resolution to the tension of the mother–child dyad and a particular solution to the threats to autonomy that derive both from the lure of love and from the intrusion of maternal power.

In our own terms, this solution is a new conception of autonomy. Autonomy is now based not on mutual recognition, pleasure, and respect but on assimilation with paternal (legitimate) power. Not only is the dialectical unity of differentiation and connection broken; the sense of difference is now secured by the introduction of a new kind of relationship.[11] In place of the lure of maternal intimacy, the son is offered, through his identification with his father, the future prospect of dominion over the maternal. No longer need his masculine identity rest on the precarious definition of male as "not-female"; rather, as discussed by Chodorow (1979, pp. 64–66) and also by Benjamin (1980), "female" is now defined as "not-male."

What neither Chodorow nor Benjamin has adequately emphasized, however, is that the significance of this paternal intervention depends not simply on the authority of the father but also on the delegitimation of maternal authority and the resultant deformation

---

11. Jessica Benjamin makes many of the same points in "The Oedipal Riddle" (1982) in language that differs from mine mainly in being somewhat stronger and more polarized. She writes: "Acceptance of the oedipal resolution means accepting this polarity. *Either* we differentiate or remain dependent; *either* we bow to reality or we remain infantile; *either* we deny our needs or we are enslaved by them. The Oedipus complex institutionalizes and reifies, gives social form and assigns gender to this polarity" (p. 202).

of mothering. Paternal authority is not simply imposed on the son; it is usually actively welcomed and even sought. Indeed, as feminists have often observed, the attractiveness of the father's power (to both sons and daughters) increases in direct proportion to the degree to which the culture devalues the mother. But mothers are not passive bystanders in this process. They react to this devaluation in ways that often exacerbate their dilemma. Mothers are actors as well as victims, just as fathers are victims as well as actors. In particular, the intrusive mother (as I will try to show) is not merely a maligning caricature of our culture or even simply a projection of the child's own fears; it is a role that many mothers unwittingly assume in reaction to their own felt powerlessness. For now, however, my principal point is that the father's authority derives its allure both from the public (and familial) legitimation of that authority *and* from the experience of real as well as fantasied maternal power. The bifurcation between paternal authority and maternal power—codified in the culture, reproduced in the family, and elaborated by the child's own fantasies—reverberates critically in the development of the child's gender identity. It is both product and critical ingredient of the entire social system constructed by—and constructing—not only fathers and sons but mothers and daughters as well. The more intrusive the mother, the more attractive the intervention of paternal authority; the more authoritarian the father, the more radical the split thus introduced between autonomy and love (especially the love of and for women[12]), or perhaps more precisely, between autonomy and dependency. And the greater the opposition between autonomy and dependency, the wider the gap between male and female. With this "static" definition of autonomy, power itself is redefined: henceforth, its legitimacy resides in the phallus. The power of the mother is neutralized first by delegitimation, and ultimately by denial.

Feminist rereadings of psychoanalytic theory make clear the ways in which such a split forecloses the possibility of recognizing the mother as a person in her own right. In both the individual and the cultural unconscious, she is a figure beclouded by simultaneous

---

12. The very real love that even the stereotypic son has for his father, tempered as it is by fear and respect, is sufficiently constrained not to seem dangerous, or in any critical way to oppose the father's autonomy.

fantasies of omnipotence and impotence.[13] Few of us ever get to know the real mother, her real power, or the real limits to her power. Instead, she survives as a specter alternately overwhelming and inconsequential. By identifying with the father, and dis-identifying from the mother, the male child attempts to remove himself from her sphere of influence altogether. Through domination, he learns to transform her omnipotence to impotence.

For the female child, however, the intervention of the father has quite different implications. Just as the son learns from his father a new meaning of masculinity, so the daughter learns a new meaning of femininity. She learns submission as the flip side of domination— as a technique of feminine seduction. She seeks in love the means of vicariously sharing in her father's authority and simultaneously usurping and extending her mother's subterraneous power. In short, she comes to internalize the specter of the mother while at the same time retaining all its ambiguities.[14]

Domination and submission are twin ploys—both substitutes for real differentiation and for dynamic autonomy. In both, the net result is curiously the same. For children of both sexes, and for most of us as adults as well,[15] the mythical power of the mother endures.[16] The

13. An excellent review of the persistence of these fantasies in feminist literature itself is provided in Chodorow and Contratto 1982.

14. For an extremely interesting discussion of the daughter's "romance" with her father, see Contratto 1983.

15. One manifestation of this confusion is the belief, widespread among women, that any inadequacies they observe in male personality are their own doing. What, they wonder, did we do to make men as they are? And what, therefore, should we be doing differently? The fact is that mothers are neither as powerful as such sentiments imply nor as impotent as the culture allows. The construction of gender (and of mothers) is not up to them alone but is a consequence of the entire psychosocial network of forces. A reciprocal manifestation of the same confusion is the absence of attention to the (positive) active role of mothers characteristic of traditional psychoanalytic theory. Autonomy, differentiation, and the incest taboo are all attributed to the agency of the father. At the same time, however, mothers can be dangerously seductive, overwhelming, or rejecting. In short, their power to do harm is seen as virtually unlimited.

16. Dorothy Dinnerstein's own tendency to slip into this fallacy is the one flaw in her otherwise brilliant analysis (1976) of the consequences of our present parenting arrangements. See Chodorow and Contratto (1982) for a more extended critique. The same problem arises in Isaac Balbus's recent work (1981), in which he undertakes the very important task of placing Dinnerstein's analysis in its social and historical context. Balbus's language itself (e.g., "Mother-Monopolized Child Rearing") is indicative of his pervasively inflationary estimation of maternal power. In turn, this preoccupation is reflected in the form of his explanatory scheme. Later on in this

eroticization of paternal power and the concomitant devaluation of maternal power may promise protection, for both daughters and sons, against the dangers embodied in the mother, but in both cases such protection has only limited psychological effectiveness. Instead of fostering true differentiation and confidence in self, it sustains ongoing anxiety about the difference between self and other by promoting the pursuit of domination in boys and of submission in girls. It also exacerbates the already visible difference between male and female, leaving daughters and sons with a legacy they will transmit as mothers and fathers. For mothers who remain fundamentally confused about the nature and limits of their own power, love itself becomes contaminated. In an attempt to assert a kind of power, they may come to confuse love with possession and intrusiveness.[17] Such confusion is in fact pandemic, and it works both ways, causing all of us sometimes to misinterpret thoughtful and responsive acts of caring as instrusions, and sometimes to misinterpret intrusiveness as evidence of love. Moreover—since mothers too are members of the same culture—their actual behavior can and often does reinforce fathers and sons in their own confusion about maternal power and love and hence in their defensive preoccupation, first with autonomy and finally with power and domination.

Conclusion

Almost certainly, human nature is such that tension between autonomy and intimacy, separation and connection, aggression and

volume (chaps. 8 and 9) I suggest that the Central Dogma of molecular biology can be seen as an example of "master-molecule theories"—theories that express a prior preoccupation with power and domination in their very structure. In this context, Balbus's theory can be seen as a minor variant of the same genre—as a kind of "mistress-molecule theory." It is striking that Balbus seeks support for his thesis, "the dominance of the mode of child rearing within symbolization," by likening the mode of child rearing to DNA: "The mode of child rearing is the social analogue of the DNA molecule: both determine the overall program or plan of development of the system of which they are a part, including the limits within which contributions to this development can be made by the other parts" (p. 349).

17. A case in point is cited by Fred Pine (1979): A young woman recently divorced described her feeling of being "annihilated": "I feel so helpless and hurt as though I can easily be destroyed if I become myself. So I just throw myself in and become the other person. Then I feel in control and powerful." About her nieces, for whom she has assumed responsibility, she says, "I take credit for the girls' accomplishments, but I blame them for their bad things. I feel in control of them. . . . It's as if they don't have minds of their own."

love, is unresolvable. But tension is not the same as opposition, and the purpose of this analysis has been to understand the ways in which our own psychosocial experience—above all, the disjunction of male from female—leads to a bifurcation between autonomy and intimacy, separation and connection, power and love. To this end, I have invoked a theory of development that describes both a cultural ideal and what continues to be—even in today's "narcissistic" culture (see Lasch 1979; also Loewald 1979, pp. 751–75)—a large part of lived human experience. But psychoanalytic theory, however descriptive, is also normative. It implies a model of parenting that has had far-reaching consequences for the ways in which mothers and fathers actually behave. In this sense, psychoanalytic theory itself plays a role in the psychosocial dynamics that lend such force to the associations of love with female "impotence" and of autonomy with male "power." Freud's own deeply pessimistic view of human nature, his radical distrust of maternal influence, and his consequent idealization of "oedipal socialization" have effectively served to "naturalize" the psychology of his age.

The revisions introduced by object relations theorists and feminist rereadings are of major significance in helping us place the phenomenology in its social context.[18] They do not, by themselves, change the phenomenology itself, but by helping to shift accepted norms, they offer the possibility of indirect change. To begin with, they facilitate the recognition and acknowledgment of other kinds of experience, kinds of experience masked by traditional psychoanalytic theory but increasingly visible to psychological observers today. In particular, the work of such psychoanalytic revisionists as Ernest Schachtel (1959),[19] John Bowlby (1969), Mary Ainsworth (1969) and most recently, Heinz Kohut (1971, 1977), who questions not only the importance of, but the very need for, an oedipal stage draws attention to the ways in which mother–infant interactions support the development of autonomy through love, attentiveness, and responsiveness. These contributions help to legitimate the work of

18. See, especially, Nancy Chodorow, "Beyond Drive Theory: Object Relations and the Limits of Radical Individualism" (unpublished manuscript) for a comprehensive treatment of this point.
19. Because of his particular interest in the interrelation of cognitive and emotional development, Schachtel's critique is taken as a starting point for the continuation of this discussion in the next essay (chap. 6).

mothers and (by implication at least) also suggest more responsive and loving roles for fathers. In this way they help to shift the balance of social values, making room for an alternative to those patterns of male and female socialization that reproduce a sexualization of aggression, power, and domination.[20] In other words, they provide support for a conception of legitimate power rooted in maternal love as well as in paternal authority: Power, as a result, can be redefined in terms of mutual interests and well-being rather than primarily in terms of conflict.[21]

Such a reconception of power, newly distinct from domination, has radical consequences for human relations, in both the private and public domains.[22] What most directly concerns us here, however, is its implications for the relations between science and nature. To explore this possibility, I have first to describe the psychological dynamics that link the desire to dominate human others with the ambition to dominate nature, and hence to a particular set of commitments for science. The next chapter is accordingly devoted to an examination of the cognitive counterparts to the emotional dynamics discussed in this essay.

20. Such a hope is supported by the anthropological findings of Peggy Reeves Sanday (as reported in Benderly 1982, pp. 40–43). From a cross-cultural analysis, Sanday concludes that societies with a high incidence of rape (about one-third of her sample) "tolerate violence and encourage men and boys to be tough, aggressive, and competitive. . . . Men mock or scorn women's practical judgment. They also demean what they consider women's work and remain aloof from childbearing and rearing. These groups usually trace their beginnings to a male supreme being" (p. 42). By contrast, Sanday's findings as summarized by Benderly lead to the conclusion that "rape-free societies glorify the female traits of nurturance and fertility. Many such peoples believe that they are the offspring of a male and female deity or that they descended from a universal womb" (p. 43). As an illustration, Benderly offers the example of the Mbuti Pygmies, who "live in cooperative small bands, men and women sharing both work and decisions. No Mbuti attempts to dominate another, nor does the group as a whole seek to dominate nature. Indeed, they refer to the forest in terms of endearment, as they would [to] a parent or lover" (p. 42).
21. The work of Jean Baker Miller, Sara Ruddick, and Nancy Hartsock argues persuasively for both the possibility and need for such a redefinition.
22. Most thoroughly explored by Hartsock 1983.

CHAPTER SIX

Dynamic Objectivity:
Love, Power, and Knowledge

> "Again I say the nearest an ordinary person gets to the essence of the scientific process is when they fall in love."
> "You fall in love with the object of your curiosity?"
> "How can you distinguish even *that*?" she objected. "The very fact that something *became* the object of your curiosity is already *process*. It is a horrible thing to say it in the way you do. Objects of curiosity? I prefer to call them things. You fall in love with a thing. Sometimes you fall in love with a fireplace, or you fall in love with a tree, and I honestly think this is the nearest ordinary people get to the genuine experience of science."
>
> GOODFIELD (1981, p. 229)

As Bacon saw so clearly, knowledge surely does bring us power. It also brings us understanding, our uniquely human way of finding connections in the world. In both these senses, the kinship between knowledge and sexuality seems to be borne out. And just as sexuality is understood differently by different people, so is knowledge. Consider the following exchange, recently reported to me by a colleague. In a class after a reading of Genesis, my colleague had asked his students to think about why it was that the word *knowledge* was used in that text simultaneously in the sexual and the epistemological sense. One student, a young man, responded, "That's obvious! Both are about power!" "Oh no," retorted another student, a young woman. "It's because both are about being in touch."

The student who could have said that both answers were right was not there. Most of us are psychosocially constituted to see love and power as irreconcilable alternatives; we do not know how to speak of them in the same breath. In the preceding essay, it was argued that this opposition between love and power, so central a theme in the emotional development of men and women, is itself responsible for the kinship of power and domination. In the present essay I will explore the cognitive expression of that same disjunction: the opposition between love and knowledge, a disjunction as central to the development of modern science as it is to the making of Western man.[1] I will argue that it is precisely this opposition— forcing a choice as it does between love and power—that makes the equation between knowledge and power a sinister one, and at the same time allows objectivity to become contaminated with domination. This last connection is emotionally constituted; it derives from the continuity between the scientist's world of objects and the "object" (better, subject) world of the child the scientist once was.

The key concept of this analysis, as in the previous essay, is psychological autonomy. But whereas the earlier discussion dealt almost entirely with emotional categories, the focus of this essay is on the interaction between emotional and cognitive experience. Accordingly, we need to look more closely at the interaction between the development of the child's (and the adult's) sense of self and sense of reality; in particular, we need to understand how the meaning we assign to objectivity reflects, and is in part determined by, our understanding of autonomy. To this end, it is useful to introduce two conceptions of objectivity—"dynamic" and "static"—parallel to the two conceptions of autonomy I discussed above. The roles played in the practice (if not in the ideology) of science by these two kinds of objectivity can in turn be seen to parallel the roles played in psychological development by dynamic and static autonomy.

I define objectivity as the pursuit of a maximally authentic, and hence maximally reliable, understanding of the world around oneself. Such a pursuit is dynamic to the extent that it actively draws on the commonality between mind and nature as a resource for

---

1. Consider, for example, the adage quoted by Bacon, "It is impossible to love and be wise" or, yet more to the point, "Amore et sapere vix Deo conceditur" (Spedding 1869, 12, p. 110).

understanding. Dynamic objectivity aims at a form of knowledge that grants to the world around us its independent integrity but does so in a way that remains cognizant of, indeed relies on, our connectivity with that world. In this, dynamic objectivity is not unlike empathy, a form of knowledge of other persons that draws explicitly on the commonality of feelings and experience in order to enrich one's understanding of another in his or her own right. By contrast, I call static objectivity the pursuit of knowledge that begins with the severance of subject from object rather than aiming at the disentanglement of one from the other. For both static and dynamic objectivity, the ambition appears the same, but the starting assumptions one makes about the nature of the pursuit bear critically on the outcome. Piaget, using slightly different terminology, reminds us:

> Objectivity consists in so fully realizing the countless intrusions of the self in everyday thought and the countless illusions which result—illusions of sense, language, point of view, value, etc.—that the preliminary step to every judgment is the effort to exclude the intrusive self. Realism, on the contrary, consists in ignoring the existence of self and hence regarding one's own perspective as immediately objective and absolute. Realism is thus anthropocentric illusion, finality—in short, all those illusions which teem in the history of science. So long as thought has not become conscious of self, it is a prey to perpetual confusions between objective and subjective, between the real and the ostensible. (1972, p. 34)

Dynamic objectivity is thus a pursuit of knowledge that makes use of subjective experience (Piaget calls it consciousness of self) in the interests of a more effective objectivity. Premised on continuity, it recognizes difference between self and other as an opportunity for a deeper and more articulated kinship. The struggle to disentangle self from other is itself a source of insight—potentially into the nature of both self and other. It is a principal means for divining what Poincaré calls "hidden harmonies and relations." To this end, the scientist employs a form of attention to the natural world that is like one's ideal attention to the human world: it is a form of love. The capacity for such attention, like the capacity for love and em-

pathy, requires a sense of self secure enough to tolerate both difference and continuity; it presupposes the development of dynamic
autonomy.

Much has been written about this kind of attention, but few
authors have granted it the degree of centrality in human development that Ernest Schachtel has. Schachtel departs pointedly from
Freud in presupposing a native, "autonomous" interest in the environment on the part of the young child that is at least as great a
spur to the emergence of self and reality as are biological needs
(1959, p. 252). This interest (or "world-openness"), he argues, is
more highly developed in humans than in other animals because of
their greater cerebralization. It is the basis of the deep pleasure the
child experiences in activity per se, in his or her spontaneous exploration of the world. In contrast to Freud (1949, p. 148), he sees
the aim of such "activity-affects" not as the "undoing" of connections,
but as the establishment of relations to one's human and natural
environment.

Schachtel's positing of a native, even primitive, impulse out-
ward, toward the world—an impulse that is neither in conflict with
relatedness nor derivative from the equally primitive impulse toward
"embeddedness"—enables him to make an important distinction. It
enables him to distinguish the feeling of "oneness" that can be established with the object of such interest from the "oceanic feeling,"
which Freud could recognize only as a regression to the early infantile state, where self and reality are not yet experienced as separate.
Such unity, Schachtel writes, "can be established not only in a re-
gressive way, by the wish to return to the womb, but also in a new
way, on a higher level of development, by loving relatedness to others and to the world" (1959, p. 182).

The perceptual tools developed to meet this interest in the
world are part of what he calls "allocentric," or other-centered, perception. They require a "complete focusing of all the perceiver's
perceptual and experiential faculties on the object, so that it is experienced in the fullest possible way"—a form of attention that, in
turn, presupposes "a temporary eclipse of all the perceiver's egocentric thoughts and strivings, of all preoccupations with self and
self-esteem, and a full turning towards the object. . . . The oneness
of allocentric perception leads not to a *loss* of self, but to a heightened feeling of aliveness" (p. 181). He cites Rilke for a description

of the state of mind necessary for such perception: "In order to have an object speak to you, you must take it for a certain time for the only one that exists, the only phenomenon which, through your devoted and exclusive love, finds itself placed in the center of the universe" (Schachtel 1959, p. 225).

For Schachtel, allocentric perception is perception in the service of a love "which wants to affirm others in their total and unique being." It is an affirmation of objects as "part of the same world of which man is part" (p. 226). In turn, and by contrast with perception that is dominated by need or self-interest (autocentric perception), it permits a fuller, more "global" understanding of the object in its own right. "This is the reason," Schachtel argues, "why love sees more than hatred. Hatred can be astute in perceiving every possibility for attack, but even though such astuteness may lead to penetrating insights . . . they always concern only part of the other and they are 'partial' to those parts which will serve as the points of attack. But hatred is unable to see its object in its totality" (p. 226).

Such intense interest in the world, and such total absorption in the object before one, is especially familiar in young children. But the capacity for employing this kind of attention in the pursuit of objective knowledge of the world requires more than interest; it requires the development of the capacity to distinguish self from other. Above all, in Schachtel's view, it requires sufficient confidence in one's own and others' abilities to satisfy one's needs to permit the employment of attention relatively free of need and anxiety. Thus, although he departs strongly from Freud in positing a native autonomous interest in the environment on the part of the child, Schachtel rejoins traditional psychoanalytic theory (and object relations theory) in his account of the development of the tools of allocentric perception. The pursuit of objectivity, in this view, has a twofold requirement: first, the survival of the child's native interest in the world, and second, the development of the capacity for focusing on objects as separate and distinct from one's own needs, desires, and individual perspective. Allocentric perception, akin to what I have called dynamic objectivity, emerges from the joining of other-centered interest and the tools of "focal attention." Conversely, its failure may result either from the inhibition of native interest, from inadequate development of the perceptual and cognitive tools that reflect the child's growing sense of autonomy, or from an interaction between the two in which interest in the world itself is subverted to the service of personal needs and anxieties.

For our purposes, it is this last developmental turn—the turn from allocentricity to "secondary autocentricity" (what would more commonly be called instrumentalism) that is of primary importance. Although Schachtel recognizes that "man could not live without the perspective of this secondary autocentricity," he goes on to say, "It can block his view of reality and lead to stagnation in a closed, autocentric world" (p. 166). The issue is whether the perception of objects is delimited by "the perspective of how they will serve a certain *need* of the perceiver, or how they can be *used* by him for some purpose" (p. 167); that is, whether the perception of objects is restricted to that of "objects-in-use." Even though for most of us science is the most obvious expression of object-centered interest, for Schachtel it is not. For him, poets and artists offer more familiar models of allocentric perception.

The reason for this is straightforward. Although he recognizes that the requirements for creativity in science and art are essentially similar, if not the same, he notes that more often scientific objects tend to be perceived primarily as "objects-in-use":

> The scientist, in these cases, looks at the object with one or more hypotheses and with the purpose of his research in mind, and thus "uses" the object to corroborate or dis-prove a hypothesis, but does not encounter the object as such, in its own fullness. Also, modern natural science has as its main goal prediction, i.e. the power to manipulate objects in such a way that certain predicted events will hap-pen. This means that only those aspects of the object are deemed relevant which make it suitable for such manipu-lation or control. . . . Thus it becomes an object-in-use. . . . In their [scientists'] attempt . . . to fit some object or phenomenon into some system, preconception, or hy-pothesis, one can often observe a blinding of themselves toward the pure and full being of the object itself. Percep-tion, then, may become almost an act of aggressive violence in which the perceiver, like Procrustes with his hapless vic-tims, cuts off those aspects of the object which he cannot use for his purposes. (p. 171)

Schachtel is describing a relation to objects that is a familiar concomitant of objectivism in general. To sever subject from object is to deny the "experiential realization of the kinship between oneself and the other" that is the essence of dynamic objectivity and that is, in Schachtel's terms, necessary to the perception of an object in its own right. It is possible to draw further and more specific connections between the vicissitudes of autonomy and its cognitive counterparts in normal behavior by looking at extreme forms of self–other interactions—forms classified as pathological. For this, I want to return to Shapiro's *Autonomy and Rigid Character* (1981), as well as to his earlier work, *Neurotic Styles* (1965). In the latter work, Shapiro described the cognitive counterparts of obsessive-compulsive and paranoid psychology; for completeness, I will add some remarks about the cognitive counterparts of sadism.

The central concern of the obsessive-compulsive is control, not so much of others as of oneself. Shapiro writes: "In his psychology, self-direction is distorted from its normal meaning of volitional choice and deliberate, purposeful action to a self-conscious directing of his every action, to the exercise, as if by an overseer, of a continuous willful pressure and direction on himself and even . . . [on] his own wants and emotions" (1965, p. 36). Under this harsh regime, attention is subject to the same kind of control as is the rest of behavior, leading to a kind of focus so intensely sharp and restricted that it precludes peripheral vision, the fleeting impression, the hunch, the over-all feeling of an object. The consequence is loss of conviction: truth is inferred rather than experienced, the basis for judgment and decisions is sought in rules rather than feeling. The obsessive-compulsive "will not say, 'It is true,' but will say something like 'It must be,' or 'It fits'" (1965, p. 50). And what does not fit is not acknowledged: "The rigid or dogmatic compulsive person simply ignores the unusual; he narrowly follows his own line of thought and goes right by anything out of the way" (1965, p. 62).

The cognitive style of the paranoid, although similar in some ways, is ultimately quite different. Grounded in the fear of being controlled by others rather than in apprehension about the loss of self-control, in the fear of giving in to others rather than to one's own unwelcome impulses, the attention of the paranoid is rigid, but it is not narrowly focused. Rather than ignore what does not fit, he or she must be alert to every possible clue. Nothing—no detail, however minor—eludes scrutiny. Everything *must* fit. The paranoid delusion suffers not from lack of logic but from unreality. Indeed, its distortion derives, at least in part, from the very effort to make all the clues fit into a single interpretation. Once accomplished, the logic is such as to leave no room for an alternative interpretation; the pieces are locked into place by the closeness of their fit. So convincing is the result that "nothing but" that interpretation can be imagined. In some ways, the paranoid resembles the quintes-sentially meticulous scientist. Normally, however, scientists recog-nize that their interpretation cannot account for every detail—that there is always, and inevitably, a certain trade-off between logic and realism.

A second, and perhaps even more crucial, distinction between paranoid and scientific perception can be found in the influence of subjective forces on the interpretation.[2] For the paranoid, interpre-tation is determined primarily by subjective need—in particular, by the need to defend against the pervasive sense of threat to one's autonomy. As in the obsessive-compulsive style, the organizing prin-ciple is vigilance—for the paranoid, vigilance against external threat; for the obsessive-compulsive, against internal threat. In both cases vigilance serves to bolster a sense of autonomy that is hypertrophied to the point of fragility—a sense of autonomy that, "because it is so frail, can be maintained only in this remarkably rigid and exagger-ated form" (Shapiro 1965, p. 80). In both cases the very fact of such vigilance—even while it sharpens some forms of perception and may be extremely useful for many kinds of scientific work—also works against all those affective and cognitive experiences that require receptivity, reciprocity, or simply a relaxed state of mind. The world of objects that emerges is a world that may be defined with extraor-dinary accuracy in many respects, but it is one whose parameters are determined principally by the needs of the observer.

A similar claim can be made for the cognitive focus that derives from a relation to objects premised on domination. For the sadistic personality, relations to others are determined primarily by the yardstick of power. The strength of one's own will is measured by another's submission. Correspondingly, understanding and compe-

2. The relevance of subjective need for a particular interpretation may be dif-ficult to judge if the interpretation is coherent. As a consequence, the falsity of a "good" paranoid interpretation may finally be evident only in the impeccability of its logic.

tence—ordinarily goals of intrinsic value—come to have value mainly to the extent that they serve to promote mastery, or domination. Perception itself is put at the service of the need to dominate. It is aimed at detecting vulnerability, points of weakness, susceptibility to attack.

But one need not look as far as the pathology of sadism for evidence of the cognitive use of perception in the interests of domination or, more generally, for defensive or offensive purposes. Such evidence is suggested by the manner in which many quite normal individuals approach the new and unknown, as well as by the language they use to describe these encounters. In particular, I have in mind the aggression expressed in the common rhetoric of science. I do not mean simply the aggression described by Schachtel, whereby the scientist "cuts off those aspects of the object which he cannot use for his purposes," but rather a kind of aggression that reflects a basic adversarial relation to the objects of study. The biologist T. S. Painter, for example, took pleasure in telling graduate students that "research is much like deer hunting. You have to be in the right place at the right time to see your prey and, of course, you must carry a loaded gun and know how to use it" (Painter 1971, p. 33). In the effort to "master" nature, to "storm her strongholds and castles," science can come to sound like a battlefield. Sometimes such imagery becomes quite extreme, exceeding even the conventional imagery of the warrior or hunter. Note, for example, the language in which one scientist describes his pursuit: "I liked to follow the workings of another mind through these minute, teasing investigations to see a relentless observer get hold of Nature and squeeze her until the sweat broke out all over her and her sphincters loosened" (quoted in Ehrenreich and English 1978, p. 69). Problems, for many scientists, are to be "attacked," "conquered," or "licked."[3] If subtler means fail, one resorts to "brute force," to the "hammer and tongs" approach. Even in gentler discourse, where problems are merely to be "solved," the underlying assumption is that in their solution, they will disappear; the process is perceived as one of clearing the field of obstacles. The complementary notion that the goal of solving problems is to reveal new questions, new perspec-

---

3. "I'll beat the bastard" was the phrase habitually employed by one scientist cited by Anthony Storr in *The Dynamics of Creation* (1972).

tives, new understanding, may also be present but is considerably less in evidence.

Few, if any, of the scientists who speak in this manner could be described as sadistic, paranoid, or obsessive-compulsive personalities. But many of the same concerns about autonomy that are manifested in acute form in pathology are, in milder form, virtually ubiquitous in the human population. If they appear especially prominent among scientists, that is because science, as described by an objectivist ideology, is a welcoming sanctuary for such concerns. A science that advertises itself by the promise of a cool and objective remove from the object of study selects for those individuals for whom such a promise provides emotional comfort. Similarly, I suggest that a science that promises power and the exercise of dominion over nature selects for those individuals for whom power and control are central concerns. And a science that conceives of the pursuit of knowledge as an adversarial process selects for those who tend to feel themselves in adversarial relation to their natural environment. The connections among these three components of scientific ideology lie not in their intellectual cohesion but in the cohesion of the emotional needs to which they appeal.

My argument, then, is that the specific kinds of aggression expressed in scientific discourse reflect not simply the absence of a felt connection to the objects one studies but also the subjective feelings many children (and some adults) experience in attempting to secure a sense of self as separate from the more immediate objects of their emotional world. The contest many scientists feel themselves engaged in, either with nature as a whole or with the particular objects they study, reflects the contest they feel themselves engaged in with human others. Similarly, the need to dominate nature is, in this view, a projection of the need to dominate other human beings; it arises not so much out of empowerment as out of anxiety about impotence. The feelings of power such domination brings are not only *like* the sense of power that can be derived from subjecting others to one's will; they are the very same feelings. In this sense, then, the dream of dominion over nature, shared by so many scientists, echoes the dream that the stereotypic son hopes to realize by identifying with the authority of his father. But such dreams are by their very nature self-limiting. They prevent the son from ever getting to know the real mother. And so, it could be argued, they similarly obstruct the scientist's efforts to know the "real" nature.

Fortunately, however, the practice of science is in fact quite different from its ideological prescriptions. Scientists differ greatly in their approaches to their subjects and in their styles of work. These differences reflect the different ways they think about nature and themselves; individual scientists give widely varying meanings to the pursuit of objectivity, paralleling the wide range of meanings attributable to autonomy. Indeed such differences are essential to the vitality of the scientific enterprise. They are also responsible for a basic thesis of this book: actual science is more faithfully described by the multiplicity of styles and approaches that constitute its practice than by its dominant rhetoric or ideology.

While some scientists see their endeavor in predominantly adversarial terms, as contests, battles, exercises in domination, others see it as a primarily erotic activity. Michael Polanyi, for example, emphasizes, instead of distance, the need to "extend our body to include [the object]—so that we come to dwell in it" (1967, p. 16). Another contemporary scientist suggests that, for the practice of scientific research, "the best analogy is always love." The reward of discovery is the feeling that "one has touched something central to another person, or to a subject, and one feels silent and grateful . . . because one was allowed to penetrate a layer of understanding which remained impenetrable to others" (Goodfield 1981, pp. 63, 69). For this scientist, understanding is not a product of cool detachment. Rather, she says, "If you really want to understand about a tumor, you've got to *be* a tumor" (p. 213). And she rejects with passion the metaphor of "putting nature on the rack and torturing the answers out of her": "I think that analogy is horrible. . . . It is like rape. Whereas in science . . . it is like the difference between rape and making love." She goes on to explain, "We are all part of nature, and if you externalize man—which is to say yourself—you are still the victim of the Inquisition, although in a different way" (p. 231).

Other such examples abound. They have been part of the tradition of modern science from the Renaissance alchemists on. But they persist throughout history only sotto voce, as minor themes made inaudible by a dominant rhetoric. Through the dynamics of simple selection, this rhetoric has had a decisive impact on the particular course that Western science has taken. In this section, I have argued that the rhetoric of domination, coercion, and mastery serves to select for a scientific community that tends toward particular emotional—and cognitive—styles. In the next section I argue for a secondary selection process in which the same rhetoric, internalized by that community, in turn selects for compatible scientific styles of work, methodologies, and even theories. Close examination of individual cases shows (Popperian claims to the contrary notwithstanding) that a recurrent and striking continuity can be seen in the way scientists work, the relation they assume to their object of study, and the theoretical orientation they favor (see Keller 1983 and chap. 9). Ideology makes itself felt principally in the process by which particular styles, methodologies, and theories come to be legitimated as "good" science. Certain theories and methods are selected as "best" by a process in which scientists collectively choose among competing methodological and theoretical candidates. The criteria for such choices are complex. Inevitably, the question is not simply which theory offers the fullest explanation, the best prediction, but also which theory best satisfies that host of unspecifiable "aesthetic" criteria (see, for example, Kuhn 1962; Hanson 1958)—including which theory is most consonant with one's implicit ideological and emotional expectations. If erotic themes have tended to be submerged in the history of science, they have been submerged by a rhetoric and ideology of aggression, which, though never binding, has been critically formative in the development of both scientists and science.

In order to get a clearer picture of the implications for science of a discourse predicated on different norms—on an ideal of dynamic rather than static objectivity—we need to examine and learn from those (generally unincorporated) traditions, which in fact can readily be found in the practice of science, even if not in its ideology. We need to pay particularly close attention to the science (both in style and substance) produced by those individuals who have seen their relation to their material in erotic rather than adversarial terms. It is to this end that, in the last chapter of this book, I return to the model provided by Barbara McClintock—perhaps the most striking exemplar of dynamic objectivity in present-day science—and attempt to identify the key elements that distinguish her vision and practice of science.

PART THREE

Theory, Practice, and Ideology in the Making of Science

I have focused so far on how science names nature—how it relates to, constructs, and contains nature. But working scientists among my readers may well question what the argument so far has to do with what, in their daily work, they actually *do*. As one physicist said in response to a lecture I recently gave, "That's all well and good, but you're not talking about science—you're talking about philosophy!"

At its best, the "doing" of science is so gripping and totally absorbing an activity that it is difficult for anyone engaged in it to step outside the demands of the particular problems under investigation to reflect on the assumptions underlying that investigation. The intensity of involvement in the immediate issues works against such reflection. Consider the kind of excitement present in laboratories at the frontiers of contemporary research, for example, in unraveling the molecular mechanisms of the immune system, an area where current developments seem truly revolutionary. Keeping track of and following all the arguments and data as they unfold, trying always to think ahead, demands total absorption; at the same time, the sense of discovering or even generating a new world intensifies excitement to a pitch not often paralleled in other academic fields. The net result is that the complementary need for reflection— for the examination of those "tacit assumptions" that unwittingly guide our reasoning—is eclipsed.

Indeed, it is rare for scientists to feel the need to reflect on their presuppositions; the success of their enterprise does not, at least in the short run, seem to require it. Some would even argue that the success of their enterprise requires that they *not* reflect on matters that would merely enmire them in ancient, fruitless disputation. Let the data speak for themselves, these scientists demand.

The problem with this argument is, of course, that data never do speak for themselves.

It is by now a near truism that there is no such thing as raw data; all data presuppose interpretation. And if an interpretation is to be meaningful—if the data are to be "intelligible" to more than one person—there must be participation in a community of common practices, shared conceptions of the meaning of terms and their relation to "objects" in the real world. In short, in science as else-where, interpretation requires the sharing of a common language.

Sharing a language means more than knowing the "right" names by which to call things; it means knowing the "right" syntax in which to pose claims and questions, and even more importantly it means sharing a more or less agreed-upon understanding of what constitute legitimate questions and meaningful answers. Every explicit question carries with it a set of implicit (unarticulated, and often unrec-ognized) expectations that limit the range of acceptable answers in ways that only a properly trained respondent will recognize. Thus, for a question such as "What accounts for X?", the range of accept-able answers is circumscribed by unspoken presuppositions about what counts as accounting—a circumscription that is assumed as a matter of course by members of a particular community.

And, as elsewhere, membership in a scientific community is most immediately indicated by the proper use of its language. An individual is most readily identified as a qualified scientist in a par-ticular field by the "right" use of vocabulary and syntax, and by a manifest appreciation of what defines a question as good and an answer as satisfying—in short, by his or her grasp of how "good and bad science get sorted out" (Watson 1966, p. 240).

Members of most communities, however, share *some* awareness of the dependence of their conceptual universe on language. What is special about many, if not all, scientific communities is precisely the widely shared assumption that the universe they study is directly accessible, represented by concepts shaped not by language but only by the demands of logic and experiment. On this assumption, "laws of nature" are beyond the relativity of language—indeed, they are beyond language: encoded in logical structures that require only the discernment of reason and the confirmation of experiment. The cor-ollary is that the descriptive language of science is transparent and neutral; it does not require examination. This assumption may be convenient for the practical demands of scientific work, but, like much of the excitement generated by that work, it depends on both the special claims science makes to truth and the kinds of truth it claims; it is in fact an inseparable part of an objectivist ideology. Translated into practice, it is also an assumption that is wondrously effective in supporting these very claims.

Confidence in the transparency of language in turn encourages the belief that one's own language is absolute. It permits the use of linguistic identifiers not only to define membership but also in support of an exclusionary understanding that secures the borders of scientific disciplines. Language, assumed to be transparent, becomes impervious. Closing the disciplinary borders against cross-traffic serves to protect the invisibility of all the inevitably self-reinforcing, even self-fulfilling, attributes of one's own language. The indifference of working scientists to (or their denial of) the self-enclosing nature of their language is no doubt helpful to the momentum of their research, but because it works to foreclose both internal awareness and external criticism of basic assumptions, it militates against deep-seated change.

The very concept of "laws of nature" is, in contemporary usage, both a product and an expression of the absence of reflectivity. It introduces into the study of nature a metaphor indelibly marked by its political origins. The philosophical distinction between descriptive and prescriptive laws is invoked to underline the neutrality of scientific description. But nonetheless, laws of nature, like laws of the state, are historically imposed from above and obeyed from below. "By those who first used the term, [laws of nature] were viewed as commands imposed by the deity upon matter, and even writers who do not accept this view often speak of them as 'obeyed' by the phenomena, or as agents by which the phenomena are produced" (OED, s.v. "law"). To be sure, there are clear and significant differences between descriptive and prescriptive laws, but at least some of these differences merely embody a presupposed ontological hierarchy. For example, whereas laws of state are open to lawful change, there is no constitutional recourse against a law of nature. Laws of nature are (at least in principle) ordinances to which matter is forever subservient. As Boyle wrote in 1665, "The wisdom of God does . . . confine the creatures to the establish'd Laws of Nature" (cited in OED, III, 17). The extreme case of the desire to turn observed regularity into law is of course the search for the one "unified" law of nature that embodies all other laws, and that hence will be immune to revision—in Bacon's language, the "summary law in which nature centres and which is subject and subordinate to God" (Spedding et al. 1869, p. 124).

So deeply entrenched is the belief in the laws (or law) of nature as the primary object of scientific inquiry that it is difficult at first glance (especially in the physical sciences), to imagine any other. Yet reflection uncovers just such an alternative. The concept of order, wider than law and free from its coercive, hierarchical, and centralizing implications, has the potential to expand our conception of science. Order is a category comprising patterns of organization that can be spontaneous, self-generated, *or* externally imposed; it is a larger category than law precisely to the extent that law implies external constraint. Conversely, the kinds of order generated or generable by law comprise only a subset of a larger category of observable or apprehensible regularities, rhythms, and patterns.[1]

Clearly, some uses of the concept of law are more constraining than others. Constraint is particularly apparent in the use of the term to refer to causal, deterministic structures—to this day, the scientific laws par excellence. Such laws imply an a priori hierarchy between structuring principle and structured matter that suggests a striking resemblance to laws of authoritarian states. Newton's laws, for example, depict a universe unfolding in strict causal sequence; once the forces are specified, its state at any future moment is completely determined by its configuration at an initial moment in time. Control, in this model, is located in the original Creation, the winding and setting of the cosmic clockwork; subsequent order is maintained by Newton's laws of motion.

In turn, the actual theoretical structures generated by a mindset looking for deterministic laws frequently exhibit internal, uni-

---

1. The distinction between law and order introduced here bears crucial kinship to the distinction between power and domination that has been made by a number of authors (see especially Hartsock 1983) as well as in an earlier essay in this volume (chap. 5). Power—which includes the various meanings of *power to, power in the interests of,* as well as *power over*—is a larger concept than domination in much the same sense that order is a larger concept than law.

directional hierarchies of their own. Thus, control may be located in a sovereign governing body, for example, in a "pacemaker" or "master molecule" (see chap. 8). The "central dogma" of molecular biology is a case in point; it depicts DNA as the executive governor of cellular organization, with unidirectional transfer of information.[2]

Our understanding of what constitutes a law (in nature as in society) is of course subject to change, and not all laws necessarily imply coercion. Certainly not all scientific laws are either causal or deterministic; they may, for example, be statistical, phenomenological, or, more simply, just the "rules of the game" (Feynman 1963, p. 2-1). But in many, perhaps most, scientific disciplines the finality of a theory continues to be measured by its resemblance to the classical laws of physics, which are both causal and deterministic.

Even in the loosest (most purely descriptive) sense of the term *law*, the kinds of order in nature that law can generate are restricted to those that can be expressed by the languages (usually mathematical) in which laws of nature are codified. All languages are capable of describing regularity, but not all perceived, and describable, regularities can be expressed in the existing vocabularies of science. Quantum mechanics (see chap. 7) provides compelling evidence for the unrealizability of a dream that can be traced all the way back to Plato—the dream of a perfect match between theory and reality—and hence subverts the possibility that natural phenomena can be fully represented by any language, much less by the existing languages of science. To assume that all perceptible regularities can be represented by current (or even by future) theory is to impose a premature limit on what is possible in nature. To further assume that all discoverable manifestations of order can be inscribed in what

2. One might argue further that the model we accept for relations among the scientific disciplines exhibits the same preoccupation with hierarchy as that manifested in the structure of theories. Theoretical sciences take precedence over empirical; and on a scale of descending primacy, we place physics at the top, chemistry below physics, and biology below chemistry. Indeed, as Sharon Traweek remarks, this hierarchical structure extends to within physics itself. She quotes one high energy physicist describing a pyramidal arrangement of disciplines, with high energy physics at the apex, other branches of physics spanning out immediately below, and applied sciences, followed by chemistry and biology, at the base of the pyramid (1984; see also 1982).

we call laws may yet more seriously circumscribe the very meaning of order and accordingly limit our potential understanding.

My argument is that even while the concept of law is subject to expansion and revision, the very word, and hence the concept also, remains tainted by its political and theological origins. An interest in order rather than law could imply far-reaching changes in our conception of science. Most directly, it would imply a shift in the focus of scientific inquiry from the pursuit of the unified laws of nature to an interest in the multiple and varied kinds of order actually expressed in nature. The former focus has historically described physics better than biology; a focus on order might look more to the biological sciences than to physics for its model. And within both physics and biology, priorities might be expected to shift away from hierarchical models of simple, relatively static systems toward more global and interactive models of complex dynamic systems.

Such a shift would imply corresponding changes in our understanding of nature and, correlatively, of the role of the scientist. "Laws" of nature name nature as blind, obedient, and simple; simultaneously, they name their maker as authoritative, generative, resourceful, and complex. Historically, the maker is God; but as discoverer and maker converge, the scientist inherits the mantle of creativity along with that of authority. In this frame, the laws imaginable by the scientist are—naturally—fully adequate to describe and contain natural order. By contrast, the conception of nature as orderly, and not merely law bound, allows nature itself to be generative and resourceful—more complex and abundant than we can either describe or prescribe. In this alternative view, nature comes to be seen as an active partner in a more reciprocal relation to an observer, equally active, but neither omniscient nor omnipotent. Such a relationship between mind and nature would require a different style of inquiry, no less rigorous but presupposing the modesty and open attentiveness that allow one to "listen to the material" (see chap. 9) rather than assuming that scientific data self-evidently "speak for themselves."

The focus on order rather than law enlarges our vision of both nature and science. It suggests a way of thinking of nature as neither bound by law nor chaotic and unruly, and of science as neither objectivist nor idiosyncratic. It suggests a science premised on respect rather than domination, neither impotent nor coercive but, as knowledge always is, inevitably empowering.

Given my earlier description of the relative imperviousness of scientific language and its consequent resistance to outside influence, one might conclude that change—of the kind I suggest or of any other kind—cannot occur. But of course change (in models, in theories, even in goals) does occur in science all the time. Physics, the most law bound of all the sciences, has undergone dramatic transformation in this century alone. I am thinking not only of the obvious revolutions introduced by relativity and quantum mechanics but also of the subtler—and perhaps finally more radical—undermining of the Newtonian paradigm that has begun as physicists turn their attention to more and more complex phenomena. In relation to these problems, traditional frames (and techniques) of analysis appear less and less appropriate. Accordingly, we begin to see the development of new mathematical techniques. These techniques make it possible to replace traditional time-dependent differential equations, which describe systems evolving in time according to specific laws, with equations better suited to describing the emergence of particular kinds of order from the varieties of order that the internal dynamics of the system can generate.

Biology too has undergone major transformation over the course of this century. In a movement that culminated in the emergence of molecular biology, an older "naturalist" tradition receded steadily before the rise of modern experimental biology. Biology claimed and won a place as a "legitimate" science, on a par with physics, in part by espousing simplicity as a primary value. But today, at the forefront of modern biology, we begin to see a resurgence of interest in complexity. As molecular biologists look more closely at higher organisms, and as they discover unsuspected complexities even in the genetics of lower organisms, the simple picture of a master blueprint residing in the cell's DNA begins to break down. The most recent developments in biology tend to confound such simple explanations and invite instead a new (for some, a renewed) interest in more dynamic, systemic, and "interactionist" descriptions, descriptions

136 THE MAKING OF SCIENCE

appropriate to a conception of nature orderly in its complexity rather than lawful in its simplicity.

Since change obviously *does* occur in science—not only in models and theories but in language itself—the question we need to ask is this: Where, given the self-enclosing inclinations of scientific ideology, does the impetus for such change arise? Some changes, such as those resulting from the development of new models and the reformulation of theories, are internally allowed and even demanded by scientific discourse. But more radical changes (changes in the discourse itself) are possible only because science is not, in fact, a closed system. Just as nature—always more abundant than its representations—inevitably transcends our laws, so the practice of science—always more abundant than its ideology—transcends its own prescriptions. On these two fronts, one between science and nature, and the other between the ideology and the practice of science, the self-definition of science remains malleable. In practice, despite all pressures toward conformity, scientists, even in the same field, speak slightly different dialects. Almost always, individuals can be found whose perspectives of and relation to nature diverge from the norm. As a consequence, even inside a relatively well-delineated community, different questions do get asked. At the same time, because order in nature is larger than the laws we can invent, different, unexpected, often seemingly anomalous or unintelligible answers are recorded—and sometimes even heard. The story of Barbara McClintock's life and work vividly exemplifies both kinds of productive mismatch (Keller 1983).

Because of these two kinds of space—the one between the laws of nature and its observable order, and the other between the ideology of science and its practice—gradual shifts in the presuppositions defining meaningful questions and satisfying answers can and do occur. But because of reluctance to acknowledge either the de facto space between theory and reality or the de facto pluralism within the scientific community, deviant questions and answers often do not get heard; the realization of change works, always, against a web of internal resistance.

A degree of closure is as necessary to the effective practice of any science as is openness, and any attempt to envision how science might be different must respect the dialectic between the two. Because of the ways in which science operates as a closed enterprise (defined by what the people we call scientists do), the possibility of envisioning a radically different science is logically foreclosed; for a "different science" to qualify as science, it would have to emerge by growth, not by discontinuity. On the other hand, because closure is not complete, because change can and does occur, it *is* meaningful to speak of how science might be different, of what shifts seem desirable, and even to explore ways by which to foster such change.

The tendency of the shifts I am advocating will by now be clear. Any such project for change requires close attention, from many different points of view, to the actual operation of the dialectic between closure and openness in the ongoing production of scientific knowledge. But because its manifestations are so largely hidden, the operation of this dialectic remains difficult to get at, and such analyses are perforce still at a rudimentary stage.

The essays that follow are intended as part of this effort; each provides an example of the interplay of theory, ideology, and practice in the production and interpretation of science. Only at the end of the last essay is gender raised as an explicit issue, but it is an implicit issue throughout all three essays. The fact is that gender ideology does not operate as an explicit force in the construction of scientific theories. Its impact (like that of ideology in general) is always indirect: in the formation and selection of preferred goals, values, methodologies, and explanations. The ideological pressures identified in each example can be seen, in the light of the essays that have gone before, as directly related to the commitment of modern science to a particular concept of masculinity.

Chapter 7, "Cognitive Repression in Contemporary Physics," was written in 1979 as a companion piece to "Gender and Science." In it I examine the debates about the interpretation of quantum mechanics that have taken place over the past half century, and I trace a continuing reluctance among contemporary physicists to accept the possibility that theory itself, even in principle, may be incapable of providing a complete representation of reality. This reluctance can be seen as evidence, on the one hand, of a deeply ingrained desire to reduce natural order to law and, on the other hand, of a continuing commitment to that very philosophy of objectivism that is widely assumed to have been negated by quantum mechanics.

Chapter 8, "The Force of the Pacemaker Concept in Theories of Aggregation of Cellular Slime Mold," offers a particularly concrete illustration, drawn from my own experience as a mathematical biologist, of the predilection for "master molecule" theories that has prevailed throughout twentieth century biology. Like chapter 7, this too can be read for the example it provides of a theoretical description emerging from an interest in order rather than law. The last chapter, on the geneticist Barbara McClintock, provides the most fully developed account of a vision of science premised on order rather than law, on respect rather than domination. Central to McClintock's vision is her insistence that good research requires, above all, the willingness to "listen to what the material has to tell you." In this essay I summarize the principal themes from the story of her life and work (Keller 1983) and discuss their relevance to the themes of gender and science.

Each of these essays describes a tension between different perspectives. However productive for change these tensions may in principle be, they remain muffled by enduring ideological commitments. The debates over the meaning of quantum mechanics continue to be stalemated, the question of pacemakers in slime mold aggregation remains unresolved, and the significance of McClintock's work, although she herself is now universally acclaimed, is still a matter of considerable dispute. The ideological commitments of modern science are deeply entrenched, and the resistance to change that they generate should not be underestimated.

CHAPTER SEVEN

Cognitive Repression in Contemporary Physics

After more than fifty years of unquestionable success as a theory, quantum mechanics remains surrounded by questions of interpretation that continue to plague both physicists and philosophers. I argue here that discussions about the meaning of quantum mechanics are stymied as a result of the failure of physicists to formulate a cognitive paradigm adequate to their theory. The conventional interpretations that they offer can be seen as inadequate in one of two ways: they retain, implicitly, one or the other of the two basic tenets of classical physics, the objectivity or the knowability of nature. What is required instead is a paradigm that on the one hand acknowledges the inevitable interaction between knower and known, and on the other hand respects the equally inevitable gap between theory and phenomena.

Piaget has invited the comparison between the historical development of scientific thought and the cognitive development of the child. Both, it is suggested, proceed through the emergence of discrete stages of structural organization, each stage bringing with it new possibilities of conceptual integration and, concurrently, the possibility of a verbal articulation of the new level of organization perceived. Prior to the establishment of a new conceptual structure, knowledge already present in nonverbal forms (in, for example, sensorimotor rather than representation schemes) finds no avenue of

A version of this chapter was first published in the *American Journal of Physics* 47 (8), August 1979, pp. 718–21; copyright © 1979 by the American Association of Physics Teachers.

expression and, to the extent that it jars with earlier established structures, demands cognitive repression. Piaget (1973, p. 249) tells us that an action schema which "cannot be integrated into the system of conscious concepts is eliminated . . . and repressed from conscious territory before it has penetrated there in any conceptualized form." Caught in a transition between stages, the child, when pressed to articulate perceptions requiring cognitive structures that are not yet available, displays confusion, denial, and avoidance—a disequilibrium strikingly reminiscent of the mechanism of affective repression.

In this paper I want to suggest that the history of science exhibits similar transitional periods, and that a particularly notable instance is to be found in contemporary physics. Today, three-quarters of a century after the Newtonian world view received its first jolts, profound confusion remains about the implications of the revolution initiated first by relativity and shortly after by quantum mechanics. This confusion is as evident among physicists as it is among the philosophical and lay public. Here, however, I focus on the confusion implicit in the minds of physicists, for it is they who have access to the knowledge that is making this revolution necessary, while philosophers and the lay public are of necessity dependent upon the physicists to communicate what it is that they know. Even among physicists, a comfortable, stable representation of the new integration required, especially by quantum mechanics, is yet to be achieved; its absence is reflected in a remarkable array of interpretations and partial accommodations, thinly veiled by a token conformity and consensus.

This last point requires emphasis and elaboration. Physicists display an extraordinary confidence in the status of quantum mechanics coupled with a general reluctance to discuss its implications. Confidence in the theoretical status of quantum mechanics is amply justified by more than fifty years of empirical support; what is at issue is the juxtaposition between the confidence in the interpretability and "sense" of this theory and the simultaneous reluctance to discuss questions of interpretation. The ongoing, often intensely heated debates about how quantum mechanics is to be interpreted are generally confined to a small group of philosophically inclined physicists. For the rest, for the majority of physicists, questions about the meaning of quantum mechanics have been "taken care of" by what is loosely called the Copenhagen Interpretation. Further inquiry is then discouraged by the implicit or explicit dual message that (1) the survival of such questions is evidence only of the inquirer's failure of understanding and (2) such questions are "just" philosophy, and hence not legitimate. If, however, one persists and attempts to pursue an understanding of *how* the Copenhagen Interpretation resolves the thorny questions raised by quantum mechanics, either through discussion or through an examination of the literature, one finds that there is not one Copenhagen Interpretation. Rather, the term seems to constitute a kind of umbrella under which a host of different, often contradictory, positions co-reside. Such a recognition provides prima facie evidence of defense and evasion; the particular substance of disagreement displayed illuminates what it is that is being evaded. In particular, what is being evaded is the need for a cognitive structure radically different from the prior existing structure. The prior structure, which I call "classical objectivism," consists of a set of formulations about the world and our relation to it as knowers that has determined the character of science since its inception. The confusion surrounding the interpretation of quantum mechanics derives from convictions that serve the function of retaining one or more components of the classical orientation.

Schrödinger (1967) has identified the two fundamental tenets of science as the beliefs that nature is (1) objectifiable and (2) knowable.[1] The first refers to the assumption of an objective reality, split off from and having an existence totally independent of us as observers. This is the principle that embodies the radical dichotomy between subject and object characteristic of the classical stance. It contains within it the implicit assumption that reality outside us is composed of objects—a rider which, although not logically necessary, is in practice an almost inevitable concomitant, if not precursor, of the classical view. The reason for this conjunction is, no doubt, that a world composed of clearly delineated objects both invites and facilitates the schism in which the subject is severed from even its own corporeal, objective existence. It is the move that

---

1. Objectifiable, here and elsewhere, means both objective, i.e., independent of our cognizance, and objectlike, hence having a well-defined position in space and time. As remarked earlier, these two meanings are almost always conjoined.

is usually held responsible for, in the words of Koyré (1968), "the splitting of our world in two."

But a world view that posits a total separation between us as subject and reality as object is by itself of no interest to science since it permits no knowledge. Science is born out of the addition of Schrödinger's second tenet—out of the confidence that nature, so objectified, is indeed knowable. Not only is a connection between us as knowers and the reality to be known here posited, but the connection posited is of an extraordinarily special nature. For most scientists it implies a congruence between our scientific minds and the natural world—not unlike Plato's assumption of kinship between mind and form (see chap. 1)—that permits us to read the laws of reality without distortion, without error, and without omission. Belief in the knowability of nature is implicitly a belief in a one-to-one correspondence between theory and reality. What makes the resultant knowledge "objective" is, perhaps even more than the ostensible split between subject and object, the separation within ourselves on which it is based. Scientific knowledge is made objective first by being dissociated from other modes of knowledge that are affectively tinged and hence tainted and, second, by being transcendentally wedded to the objects of nature. This felicitous marriage between the scientific mind and nature is consummated, not by worldly intercourse, but by a form of direct communion with nature, or with God, for which the scientific mind is uniquely, and unquestionedly, equipped.[2]

The loneliness that others might find in a world in which subject and object are split apart is mitigated, for the scientist, by his special access to the transcendent link between the two. The conflicting impulses implicit in these two components of objectivism find exquisite resolution in the classical Newtonian world view. Their intermingling confounds our efforts to sort out the dual aims of power and transcendence evident in the scientific endeavor; it leads simultaneously to the romantic view of the scientist as religious mystic—celibate, austere, and removed from the world of the senses—

---

2. Newton, e.g., was sometimes quite explicit in articulating the consonance between scientific thought and God's "Sensorium": "There is a Being incorporeal, living, intelligent, omnipresent who in infinite space, as it were in his sensory, sees things intimately . . . of which things the images only . . . are there seen and beheld by that which in us perceives and thinks" (*Opticks*, 3d ed. London 1921, p. 344).

and to the technological view of science as dedicated to mastery, control, and the domination of nature. It would seem that an analysis of their primitive sources might permit an appreciation of the ways in which these impulses collaborate to produce the character (collective and individual) of the scientific enterprise. The possibilities of such an analysis tease the imagination, and I will have a little more to say about this later. First, however, I want to try to spell out the ways in which these two components have evolved under the impact of quantum mechanics.

Physical theory provides a description of reality by designating the state of the system, a system being a single particle or group of particles. In classical theory, the state of a system is a point in phase space, that is, the position and momentum of the particle or particles. Quantum mechanics precludes such a specification and offers in its stead a vector in Hilbert space, or the wave function, which contains the maximal information possible about the state of the system. It is the character of this description that generates the familiar concepts of wave particle duality, complementarity, and uncertainty. The wave function is not a point in space but rather a distribution of points. It does not in general prescribe a definite value for the position, momentum, or for that matter, any observable aspect of the system, but only a "probability amplitude." Furthermore, the more precise the specification provided by the wave function for one observable (for example, position), the less precise its specification for the complementary observable (for example, momentum). Questions of interpretation arise out of the need to articulate the relation between this description and the actual system. In classical theory, little difficulty arose from regarding the state of the system as simultaneously and equally an attribute of the theoretical description and of the system itself. In quantum mechanics, however, the very character of the description provided by theory makes it extremely difficult, if not impossible, to maintain this identification. In spite of the fact that the wave function of a system, prior to measurement, fails to prescribe a definite value of the observable being measured, any measurement invariably yields a definite position, momentum, spin, and so forth. The state of the system is quite definite after the measurement with respect to the variable being measured, however indefinite it may have been before. The wave function is said to have "collapsed." It is the need

to interpret this statement that generates the major problems and
confusions that surround the debates over quantum mechanics.

One especially dramatic form in which such problems find
expression is that of Schrödinger's cat, whose hypothetical death is
triggered, Rube Goldberg style, by the decay of a radioactive nu-
cleus. The time of decay, and hence the time at which the cat is
killed, is indeterminate; theory can provide no more than a "probability amplitude" for decay at any particular time. When enough
time has elapsed to yield a probability of decay of one half, the wave
function for the system will be a "superposition" of states in which
live cat and dead cat are mixed in equal proportions. The ostensible
paradox emerges from the evident fact that any particular cat must
be either alive or dead, while the wave function represents both.
Schematically, one can point to two classes of errors that persist, in
varying degrees and combinations, in the effort to resolve this paradox.

The first error resides in what can be called the statistical interpretation, in which it is asserted that the state of the system is a
description only of a conceptual ensemble of similarly prepared systems; no knowledge about an individual system is claimed or, indeed, is considered possible. Any particular cat of Schrödinger's is,
at any time, either alive or dead. The wave function, however, describes only an ensemble of such cats. Its "collapse" is viewed as
being no different from the "collapse" of any probability distribution
function in the face of new knowledge. This view, while avoiding
many pitfalls which other views leave themselves open to, permits
the retention of the classical view of the particle as having a well-
defined position and momentum (and hence a classical trajectory),
albeit unknowable. That is, the objectifiability of a one-to-one mapping of that reality onto our theoretical constructs is abandoned. The
necessity of rooting the correspondence between theory and reality
in the empirical, experiential process of observation is acknowledged, and results of this experience force us to give up our prior
belief that the fit can be made perfect.

This is a radical posture insofar as it represents a decisive developmental step beyond the belief in the existence of a direct correspondence unmediated by actual experience—a belief that I think
ought properly be called magical. It is not radical enough insofar as
it fails to give up the picture of reality that had emerged under the

classical regime. In this interpretation, the attribution of wavelike properties to the particles themselves is, quite correctly, understood to be a mistake. The wavelike properties are acknowledged to belong to (that is, emerge from) the process of observation. To quote one physicist, "Students should not be taught to doubt that electrons, protons, and the like are particles. . . . The wave cannot be observed in any other way than by observing particles" (Mott 1964, p. 409). What is not acknowledged here is that the same statement can and must be made of its particle-like properties. They too emerge only from the process of observation. In giving up the comfortable belief that the wave function provides a theoretical description of an individual system, adherence to the classical picture of this system leads to the extreme statement that quantum mechanics has nothing at all to say about the individual system (see, for example, Peres 1974, p. 886). It is in this last statement that the inadequacy of the statistical interpretation specifically resides. The wave function, or quantum-mechanical state, represents a picture not of the individual system itself but of the associated processes of preparation and detection of either an individual system or an ensemble of systems, and is capable of yielding quite definite statements about an individual system. This the statistical interpretation does not account for.[3]

The second, and far more common, kind of error that permeates interpretations of quantum mechanics lies in attributing a kind of objective, material reality to the wave function itself. This mistake resides implicitly in all views that claim that the quantum-mechanical state constitutes a complete and exhaustive description of the system. It expresses itself in statements which assert that a system "has state 'psi,'" or that "there exists a state or wave function," implying that in determining this state, one is measuring something which is an intrinsic or objective property of the system rather than that of the measurement process itself. This posture has a long history, dating from Schrödinger's most primitive view of the wave function as a kind of material distribution of the particle. It lies behind the conception of the particle or system as actually possessing

---

3. Although not generally realized, it is in fact possible to formulate quantum mechanics entirely in terms of yes–no judgments, without ever making reference to probabilities. See, e.g., D. Finkelstein, Trans. N.Y. Acad. Sci. 621 (1964).

wavelike properties, and leads to seeing the "collapse" of the wave function as a real paradox. Contained in the surprise that the wave function can "collapse" from a distribution of values to a particular value is the belief that the system itself undergoes, in the process, a similar collapse. If so, the question of how this is accomplished is indeed a difficult one, and has understandably plagued discussions of quantum mechanics since its inception.

Many authors have suggested that it is the act of observation which "causes" the collapse of the wave function, thus inviting further debate about what it is in the act of observation that triggers this reduction. Wigner (1975) has gone so far as to assert that it is the very act of knowing that exerts what is now perceived as a physical effect on the system, forcing it into a state with definite position, momentum, or spin. He argues that, since it is well known in physics that to every action there is a reaction, it would be unreasonable to suppose that phenomena can exert an influence on our consciousness without our consciousness in turn exerting an effect on the phenomena. Thus Schrödinger's cat would be induced into a state of being definitely alive or dead by the very act of knowing.

This is the most extreme of a range of positions that are sometimes called the "subjective" interpretations of quantum mechanics—all loosely associated with the Copenhagen Interpretation. *Subjective* in these interpretations means that the classical conviction of the independence of the object from the subject is given up. Experience demonstrates the failure of the classical dichotomy; subject and object are inevitably, however subtly, intertwined. So far so good. The difficulties arise in the tendency to overestimate our capacity to describe that interaction. That is, if we are unwilling to acknowledge aspects of reality not contained in the theoretical description, it is the system itself, for example, the electron, which must bend, twist, or collapse in response to our observation. Such a system cannot be a classical particle; classical particles are not "spread out," nor do they "collapse." We give up the classical picture but impose on reality the picture of our theoretical description, saying, implicitly, that the system *is* this peculiar object, the wave function. In short, the subject–object dichotomy is relinquished, but the attachment to a one-to-one correspondence between reality and theory is not. In these interpretations, belief in the "knowability" of nature is retained at the expense of its "objectifiability." Reality then, of necessity, takes on rather bizarre properties in this effort to make it conform to theory, leaving very few content.

In an effort to escape from this quagmire, theorists have proposed more and more outlandish alternatives. As with the child caught between cognitive paradigms, the ingenuity that physicists have displayed is quite impressive. Thus, for example, a number of physicists have expressed enthusiasm for a resolution called "The Many Worlds Interpretation of Quantum Mechanics," in which the universe is seen as continually splitting into a multitude of mutually unobservable but equally real worlds. In each world, measurement yields a definite result. Schrödinger's cat is unequivocally alive in some, dead in others. All that remains equivocal is in which world we shall find ourselves. This interpretation demonstrates remarkable ingenuity in that it manages to retain confidence in both the object reality of the system and its literal correspondence with theory. Of course, a price has been paid—namely, the price of seriousness.

Finally, all this confusion can be avoided by dismissing the questions altogether. The strong positivist ethos surrounding contemporary science makes it possible for some, perhaps most, physicists to limit the definition of reality to the body of theoretical and empirical knowledge at our disposal and to declare as meaningless all questions about the actual nature of the systems being studied and our relation to those systems. Without embarking on a critique of this position, I wish only to point out what is fairly obvious, namely, that it provides an extraordinarily convenient cover under which all sorts of prior beliefs about the world and its relation to science can, and do, subterraneously reside. It is too bad that we do not permit the child similar license to respond to Piaget's telling questions (questions that cannot be handled within an existing cognitive paradigm) by saying simply, "Your questions are meaningless."

At this point it must be asked why the classical paradigm is so difficult to give up in toto. Piaget attributes cognitive repression to the familiarity and success of older, established structures, and no doubt he is at least partly right. Certainly, the classical tenets of science have proved extraordinarily successful, and continue, in most areas of science, to do so. It seems, however, that the confusion that has for so long been evidenced in discussions about quantum mechanics, and the intense emotion such discussions can evoke, suggest that more is at stake than simply the comfort and success of an older paradigm. The great weakness of Piaget's developmental system is his failure to include any consideration of the impact of affective components on the developmental process. Egocentricity, omnipotence, and object permanence are all terms with profound meaning in the domain of affective relations as well as of cognitive relations. Although some attempt has been made to integrate the psychoanalytic understanding of affective development with Piaget's understanding of cognitive development, this remains an area in need of more research. A few comments may nevertheless be in order.

We know both from Piaget and from psychoanalysis that the capacity for objective thought and perception is not inborn but, rather, is acquired as part of the long and painful struggle for psychic autonomy—a state never entirely free of ambiguity and tension. The internal pressure to delineate self from other (a pressure exacerbated by the historical emphasis on ego autonomy) leaves us acutely vulnerable to anxiety about wishes or experiences that might threaten that delineation. We know further that such anxiety can sometimes be allayed by the imposition of an excessively delineated structure on one's emotional and cognitive environment. It would seem, therefore, that objectification in science may serve a related function. The severance of subject from object, as well as the insistence on the premise that science is affect-free, may derive in part from a heavily affect-laden motive for separateness and may serve to buttress a sense of autonomy. If so, then the continuing adherence to the belief in the objectifiability of nature would be assisted by the emotional functions served by this belief.

Similarly, the attachment to the premise that nature is "knowable" can also be viewed in psychological terms. The ideal of a perfect congruence between us as knowers and an objective reality to be known is strikingly reminiscent of other ideas—ubiquitous among children—which we call magical. It represents a continuing belief in omniscience, now translated out of the domain of magic into the domain of science. Based on a vision of transcendent union with nature, it satisfies a primitive need for connection denied in another realm. As such, it militates against the acceptance of a more realistic, more mature, and more humble relation to the world in which the boundaries between subject and object are acknowledged to be never quite rigid and in which knowledge of any sort is never quite

COGNITIVE REPRESSION IN CONTEMPORARY PHYSICS   149

total. In such a frame, I suggest that the antinomies of quantum mechanics would no longer be so problematic.

Both tenets, knowability and objectifiability, need to be relinquished. The testimony of quantum mechanics is eloquent: however successful these tenets have been in the past, they are no longer adequate. Yet this testimony remains obscured by interpretations that implicitly attempt to retain some residue of the classical paradigm. Each of the two dominant schools of interpretation—the statistical and the Copenhagen—suffers from inadequacies that are evident to proponents of the other, and debate between the two continues. The failure to reach a resolution of this debate reflects the difficulties even quantum physicists have in completely relinquishing some adherence to at least one of the two basic premises of classical physics: the objectifiability and knowability of nature. The vision implicit in quantum mechanics still awaits representation in a cognitive paradigm yet more radical than any that the conventional interpretations have offered us.

CHAPTER EIGHT

The Force of the Pacemaker Concept in Theories of Aggregation in Cellular Slime Mold

A given problem may attract a scientist for any number of reasons. In turn, those reasons, or interests, influence the manner in which he or she deals with the problem. It is appropriate, therefore, that I begin with a description of my own initial interest in the problem of slime mold aggregation.

That interest began more than ten years ago, when, working as a mathematical biologist, I had become preoccupied by what might be regarded as the fundamental question of developmental biology: the origin of structure, or the origin of difference in an initially undifferentiated system. All cells of a complex organism derive from the same initial cell and presumably, therefore, have the same genetic material. What, then, determines the differential expression of a given genetic complement in cells that take on widely varying structural and functional characteristics? Just at this time, I discovered an old and at the time little known paper by Alan Turing (1952). Turing demonstrated that a hypothetical system of interacting chemicals, reacting and diffusing through space, could generate a regular spatial structure which, he speculated, would provide a basis for subsequent morphogenetic development.

What was appealing about this view was that it offered a way

A version of this chapter was first published in Evelyn Fox Keller, *Perspectives in Biology and Medicine*, 26, 4 (Summer 1983), pp. 515–21; edited by Richard L. Landau; copyright © 1983 by the University of Chicago.

out of the infinite regress into which thinking about the development of biological structure so often falls. That is, it did not presuppose the existence of a prior pattern, or difference, out of which the observed structure could form. Instead, it offered a mechanism for self-organization in which structure could emerge spontaneously from homogeneity.

Thinking like a mathematician and not like a biologist, I found it natural to look for a system that would lend itself to such an analysis, that is, that might provide a demonstrable instance of such self-organizing principles. At this time I met Lee Segel, who introduced me to the problem of aggregation in the cellular slime mold *Dictyostelium discoideum*. Dictyostelium has the remarkable property of existing alternatively as single cells or as a multicellular organism. As long as there is enough food around, the single cells are self-sufficient, growing and dividing by binary fission. But, when starved, these cells undergo internal changes that lead to their aggregation into clumps which, as they grow bigger, topple over and crawl off as slugs. Under appropriate conditions of light, humidity, and pH, the slug stops, erects a stalk, and differentiates into stalk and spore cells; the spores subsequently germinate into single-celled amoebas.

The onset of aggregation is the first visible step in the process that eventually leads to the cellular differentiation observed in the multicellular organism. Prior to aggregation, no difference among cells is apparent. But once it occurs, aggregation itself induces a differential environment that could presumably be the basis of subsequent differentiation. The question is, What triggers the aggregation?

It was already known that the individual cells produce an acrasin (identified as cyclic AMP) to which they are chemotactically sensitive as well as an acrasinase that degrades the acrasin. Following in the spirit of Turing, Segel and I examined the spatial stability of a homogeneous field of undifferentiated cells interacting through the production and degradation of, and chemotaxis to, acrasin. We showed that the conditions for instability, for the onset of aggregation, would be met by an increase of individual cellular production of acrasin and/or chemotactic sensitivity *without prior differentiation*. That these changes actually take place was independently corroborated by experiment (Bonner et al. 1969).

Unfortunately, because our analysis was linear, we could comment only on the onset of instability. Furthermore, the model itself
was highly oversimplified. In particular (and this proved to be a fatal
flaw), we ignored the fact that the aggregation process is not steady
but proceeds in pulses. Although this simplification was made in the
interests of mathematical tractability, we hoped that the oscillatory
behavior might emerge as a second-order instability. Our main purpose was not to provide a detailed accounting of the aggregation
process but rather to offer an alternative to the widespread view that
special (sometimes called founder) cells were needed to initiate aggregation. Specifically, we sought an alternative to the picture that
Shaffer had earlier proposed (1962) of aggregation resulting from the
emission of periodic signals by a central cell (a founder or pacemaker
cell) and relayed through the medium by the rest of the cells. There
were at least two reasons for seeking an alternative to this picture.
First, no evidence for such "special" cells existed. Second, it was
known that when the centers of aggregation patterns are removed,
new centers form—that is, aggregation is undisturbed.

Nonetheless, shortly after Segel and I published our model
(Keller and Segel 1970), the initiator cell view was revived by Cohen
and Robertson (1971a) with a considerably more detailed description
of the relay of signals emitted by pacemaker cells through a population of relay competent cells. They supported this description with
a discrete model (1971b) to demonstrate its feasibility and embarked
on a series of experiments designed to measure the temporal properties of the signal. These properties became the central focus of
research for many investigators. Still photographs were produced
exhibiting concentric and spiral wave patterns (strikingly like those
of the Zhabotinsky chemical reaction); time-lapse photography
showed outward-moving waves as the cells themselves moved in-
ward. But preoccupation with the phenomenology of aggregation
waves obscured rather than addressed the key distinction between
the two models: the existence or nonexistence of predetermined initiator or pacemaker cells. For reasons that are still not clear to me,
the question that I had considered the central issue—the question
of what triggers the initial differentiation—was *not* the question of
interest to most biologists or mathematical biologists working on the
subject. In fact, the pacemaker view was embraced with a degree
of enthusiasm that suggests that this question was in some sense

foreclosed. The assumption of pacemaker cells was felt to be so natural, it so readily explained the phenomena, that the question I had begun with simply disappeared.

In the years that followed, the word *pacemaker* crept into the literature as a fait accompli. Despite the continuing lack of evidence for or against their existence, researchers selected for mutants that produced fewer or no "pacemakers" and even invoked the case of cellular slime mold to contrast with other systems exhibiting similar phenomenology but where the question of the existence of centers or pacemakers was at least open (most notably, the Zhabotinsky reaction [Winfree 1980]). In fact, the force of the pacemaker concept has been so great as occasionally to spill over and influence the way people think about the Zhabotinsky reaction itself. In a recent talk on the dangers of analogical thinking in biology, Nancy Kopell (1980) remarked:

> In the slime mold case, there are cells with special prop-
> erties which govern the behavior of cells around them.
> [Later in the same talk, Kopell acknowledged the uncer-
> tainty of this assumption.] These are the cells at the center
> of the aggregating clump which give off periodic pulses of
> cyclic AMP. As soon as one is under the influence of that
> analogy, it is almost inevitable that the centers of the Zha-
> botinski patterns would be seen in this light. And indeed,
> they are often called pacemakers in the literature; at least
> one set of authors refers to communication between the
> center and the outer rings in terms of "chemical radio
> waves." For slime mold, this makes good physiological
> sense; for the Zhabotinski reagent, it is mysticism. For what
> could possibly be the radio tower? Some experimenters
> claim to produce the patterns without any heterogeneities
> at the centers. Others produce more target patterns simply
> by sprinkling in floor dust, or as one experimenter has been
> known to do, ruffling his beard over the reagent.

The fact of the matter is, however, that even though they may make physiological sense, "radio towers" are no more demanded by the evidence in slime mold than they are in the Zhabotinsky reaction.

At the time the pacemaker view became prevalent, I was simply perplexed. But other interests, especially in the history and philosophy of science, drew me away from mathematical biology. In my biographical study of the cytogeneticist Barbara McClintock (1983), I became interested in the force that particular kinds of models have over the understandability and, hence, acceptability of different theories in biology. The McClintock story is in part a story of the conflict between a community that became increasingly committed to the view of genes, and later of DNA, as the central actor in the cell—that which governs all other cellular processes—and an individual whose own view was that genes, or DNA, constitute only one part of the cell. These two views have a long history in biology, especially in genetics; but, as David Nanney wrote more than twenty-five years ago, "The emphasis has been very strongly in favor of one of these. . . . The first we will designate as the 'Master Molecule' concept. . . . . This is in essence the theory of the Gene, interpreted to suggest a totalitarian government. . . . The second concept we will designate as the 'Steady State' concept. By this term . . . we envision a dynamic self-perpetuating organization of a variety of molecular species which owes its specific properties not to the characteristic of any one kind of molecule, but to the functional interrelationships of these molecular species" (Nanney 1957, p. 136). In order to understand the failure of the biological community to comprehend McClintock's early work on genetic transposition, I saw increasingly clearly that I had to think about the role that prior commitments (to hierarchy, in this case) play in the history of the development of scientific theories.

Slime mold aggregation was far from my mind when I received a call from a newcomer to the field of mathematical biology who had come across the paper Segel and I had written on this subject, but had not been able to find either any serious critique or any follow-up. He wanted to know what was going on. Why, as he put it, had our paper been suppressed?

Well, our paper had clearly not been suppressed. But this question was nonetheless a provocative one, and it obliged me to wonder about the role that prior extrascientific commitments played in the fate of our own early model. In the light of this concern, my point becomes an obvious one: I am suggesting that the story of pacemakers in slime mold aggregation provides an unusually simple instance of the predisposition to kinds of explanation that posit a single central governor; that such explanations appear both more natural and conceptually simpler than global, interactive accounts; and that we need to ask why this is so. To the extent that such models also lend themselves more readily to the kinds of mathematics that have been developed, we further need to ask, What accounts for the kinds of mathematics that have been developed? Mathematical tractability is a crucial issue, and it is well known that, in all mathematical sciences, models that are tractable tend to prevail. But might it not be that prior commitments (ideological, if you will) influence not only the models that are felt to be satisfying but also the very analytic tools that are developed?

The Keller-Segel model was clearly inadequate in its original form, primarily because of its lack of a nonlinear analysis. In addition, it failed to incorporate the more complex internal dynamics of the individual cells that are linked to the oscillatory nature of cyclic AMP production. But ten years ago, we did not have the mathematical techniques for such an analysis. In the intervening period, however, we have witnessed a tremendous growth in the study of nonlinear equations, most notably in the study of reaction-diffusion equations. As a result of this effort, it is now possible to pursue the analysis necessary to understand the interaction between the production and diffusion of acrasin and cellular chemotaxis. Indeed, some of this analysis has now been carried out by Marcus Cohen and Pat Hagan (1981).

Cohen and Hagan's analysis is based on a model of cyclic AMP production in single cells that Cohen had previously developed. From this model, steady-state, excitable, and oscillatory dynamics can be seen to emerge for different values of an internal parameter that can be loosely linked to the degree of cell starvation. The system becomes multicellular, and spatial, with the addition of the diffusion of extracellular cyclic AMP. Through their analysis of the resulting spatiotemporal equations, Cohen and Hagan were able to show the emergence of spirals, target patterns, and streams—all corresponding to different values of the cellular control parameter. The crucial point is this: The different morphologies appear through successive bifurcations of a single reaction-diffusion system and do not require the expression of new genetic information. Outgoing concentric waves are generated by local maxima in the frequency of cyclic AMP oscillations; frequency is thought to vary with the internal parameter in a manner that is not made explicit in the model. The motion of the amoebas themselves, essentially decoupled from the chemical system in this model, follows the gradients of cyclic AMP generated by the wave patterns.

The Cohen–Hagan model has the great advantage of dispensing with the need for prior differentiation. Cells that are, for whatever reason, in a state of greater starvation become likely candidates for aggregation centers.[1] These cells do not need to be pacemakers. They might, nonetheless, continue to be regarded as such. History suggests that merely demonstrating the superfluity of pacemakers may not be sufficient to dislodge the concept itself from the hold it has on our thinking.

My own reservation about this otherwise remarkable piece of analysis has to do with the assumption, built into the base of the Cohen-Hagan model, that cellular motion can be regarded as a second-order phenomenon. The authors begin with the claim that "the chemical waves underlie and govern the cell movement." While this assumption may be partly justified by the fact that cell velocity is small compared with wave velocity, it is also important to note that it is made in part because the mathematics that has been developed for reaction-diffusion systems is not readily adapted to include chemotaxis. To the extent that we focus on the nature of the instability that gives rise to centers, the cells and their motion are likely to be essential considerations. Hagan and Cohen do not discuss this issue, but we may speculate that local spatial inhomogeneities—for example of the kind that come out of the simple Keller–Segel model—might, by the simple accumulation of cells and the consequent local exhaustion of food,[2] be the mechanism that triggers the early local onset of oscillation. The importance of the cell–chemical interaction is still an open question, but perhaps we should be wary of beginning an analysis with the assumption that the chemical system "governs" the cellular system.

1. A similar approach was taken by Hagan (1981) and Kopell (1981) for the Zhabotinsky reaction, where, as here, different morphologies were shown to emerge from differences in the level of a parameter rather than differences in kind. The former are relatively easy to account for, e.g., the gas sticking to the surface of virtually any solid particle can locally change the frequency of the chemical oscillation, thereby giving rise to target patterns.

2. I am indebted to Nancy Kopell for this suggestion.

More generally, I am suggesting that we might learn from the pacemaker story to be wary of imposing causal relations on all systems that seem by their very nature to be more complexly interactive. As scientists, our mission is to understand and explain natural phenomena, but the words *understand* and *explain* have many different meanings. In our zealous desire for familiar models of explanation, we risk not noticing the discrepancies between our own predispositions and the range of possibilities inherent in natural phenomena. In short, we risk imposing on nature the very stories we like to hear.

CHAPTER NINE

A World of Difference

O Lady! We receive but what we give,
And in our life alone does Nature live:
Ours is her wedding garment, ours her shroud!

SAMUEL TAYLOR COLERIDGE, "Dejection: An Ode"

If we want to think about the ways in which science might be different, we could hardly find a more appropriate guide than Barbara McClintock. Known to her colleagues as a maverick and a visionary, McClintock occupies a place in the history of genetics at one and the same time central and peripheral—a place that, for all its eminence, is marked by difference at every turn.

Born in 1902, McClintock began in her twenties to make contributions to classical genetics and cytology that earned her a level of recognition few women of her generation could imagine. Encouraged and supported by many of the great men of classical genetics (including T. H. Morgan, R. A. Emerson, and Lewis Stadler), McClintock was given the laboratory space and fellowship stipends she needed to pursue what had quickly become the central goal of her life: understanding the secrets of plant genetics. She rejected the more conventional opportunities then available to women in science (such as a research assistantship or a teaching post at a woman's college)[1] and devoted herself to the life of pure research. By the mid 1930s, she had already made an indelible mark on the history of genetics. But the fellowships inevitably ran out. With no job on the horizon, McClintock thought she would have to leave science. Mor-

1. For an excellent overview of the opportunities available to women scientists in the 1920s and 1930s, see Rossiter 1982.

gan and Emerson, arguing that "it would be a scientific tragedy if her work did not go forward" (quoted in Keller 1983, p. 74), prevailed upon the Rockefeller Foundation to provide two years interim support. Morgan described her as "the best person in the world" in her field but deplored her "personality difficulties": "She is sore at the world because of her conviction that she would have a much freer scientific opportunity if she were a man" (p. 73). Not until 1942 was McClintock's professional survival secured: at that time, a haven was provided for her at the Carnegie Institution of Washington at Cold Spring Harbor, where she has remained ever since. Two years later she was elected to the National Academy of Science; in 1945 she became president of the Genetics Society of America.

This dual theme of success and marginality that poignantly describes the first stage of McClintock's career continues as the leitmotif of her entire professional life. Despite the ungrudging respect and admiration of her colleagues, her most important work has, until recently, gone largely unappreciated, uncomprehended, and almost entirely unintegrated into the growing corpus of biological thought. This was the work, begun in her forties, that led to her discovery that genetic elements can move, in an apparently coordinated way, from one chromosomal site to another—in short, her discovery of genetic transposition. Even today, as a Nobel laureate and deluged with other awards and prizes for this same work, McClintock regards herself as, in crucial respects, an outsider to the world of modern biology—not because she is a woman but because she is a philosophical and methodological deviant.

No doubt, McClintock's marginality and deviance is more visible—and seems more dramatic—to her than to others. During the many years when McClintock's professional survival seemed so precarious, even her most devoted colleagues seemed unaware that she had no proper job. "What do you mean?," many of them asked me. "She was so good! How could she not have had a job?" Indeed, as Morgan himself suggested, her expectation that she would be rewarded on the basis of merit, on the same footing as her male colleagues, was itself read as a mark of her ingratitude—of what he called her "personality difficulties."

When discussing the second stage of her career, during which her revolutionary work on genetic transposition earned her the reputation more of eccentricity than of greatness, her colleagues are

likely to focus on the enduring admiration many of them continued
to feel. She, of course, is more conscious of their lack of compre-
hension and of the dismissal of her work by other, less admiring,
colleagues. She is conscious, above all, of the growing isolation that
ensued.

Today, genetic transposition is no longer a dubious or isolated
phenomenon. As one prominent biologist describes it, "[Transpos-
able elements] are everywhere, in bacteria, yeast, *Drosophila*, and
plants. Perhaps even in mice and men." (Marx 1981, quoted in Keller
1983, p. 193). But the significance of transposition remains in considerable dispute. McClintock saw transposable elements as a key to
developmental regulation; molecular biologists today, although much
more sympathetic to this possibility than they were twenty, or even
ten, years ago, are still unsure. And in evolutionary terms, Mc-
Clintock's view of transposition as a survival mechanism available to
the organism in times of stress seems to most (although not to all)
pure heresy.

My interest here, as it has been from the beginning, is less on
who was "right" than on the differences in perceptions that underlay
such a discordance of views. The vicissitudes of McClintock's career
give those differences not only special poignancy but special importance. In *A Feeling for the Organism: The Life and Work of Barbara McClintock* (Keller 1983), I argued that it is precisely the
duality of success and marginality that lends her career its significance to the history and philosophy of science. Her success indis-
putably affirms her legitimacy as a scientist, while her marginality
provides an opportunity to examine the role and fate of dissent in
the growth of scientific knowledge. This duality illustrates the diversity of values, methodological styles, and goals that, to varying
degrees, always exists in science; at the same time, it illustrates the
pressures that, to equally varying degrees, operate to contain that
diversity.

In the preface to that book (p. xii), I wrote:

> The story of Barbara McClintock allows us to explore the
> condition under which dissent in science arises, the function
> it serves, and the plurality of values and goals it reflects. It
> makes us ask: What role do interests, individual and col-
> lective, play in the evolution of scientific knowledge? Do all

scientists seek the same kinds of explanations? Are the kinds
of questions they ask the same? Do differences in methodology between different subdisciplines even permit the
same kinds of answers? And when significant differences do
arise in questions asked, explanations sought, methodologies
employed, how do they affect communication between scientists? In short, why could McClintock's discovery of transposition not be absorbed by her contemporaries? We can
say that her vision of biological organization was too remote
from the kinds of explanations her colleagues were seeking,
but we need to understand what that distance is composed
of, and how such divergences develop.

I chose, in effect, not to read the story of McClintock's career
as a romance—neither as "a tale of dedication rewarded after years
of neglect—of prejudice or indifference eventually routed by courage
and truth" (p. xii), nor as a heroic story of the scientist, years "ahead
of her time," stumbling on something approximating what we now
know as "the truth." Instead, I read it as a story about the languages
of science—about the process by which worlds of common scientific
discourse become established, effectively bounded, and yet at the
same time remain sufficiently permeable to allow a given piece of
work to pass from incomprehensibility in one era to acceptance (if
not full comprehensibility) in another.

In this essay, my focus is even more explicitly on difference
itself. I want to isolate McClintock's views of nature, of science, and
of the relation between mind and nature, in order to exhibit not
only their departure from more conventional views but also their
own internal coherence. If we can stand inside this world view, the
questions she asks, the explanations she seeks, and the methods she
employs in her pursuit of scientific knowledge will take on a degree
of clarity and comprehensibility they lack from outside. And at the
heart of this world view lies the same respect for difference that
motivates us to examine it in the first place. I begin therefore with
a discussion of the implications of respect for difference (and complexity) in the general philosophy expressed in McClintock's testimony, and continue by discussing its implications for cognition and
perception, for her interests as a geneticist, and for the relation
between her work and molecular biology. I conclude the essay with
a brief analysis of the relevance of gender to any philosophy of difference, and to McClintock's in particular.

Complexity and Difference

To McClintock, nature is characterized by an a priori complexity that vastly exceeds the capacities of the human imagination. Her recurrent remark, "Anything you can think of you will find,"[2] is a statement about the capacities not of mind but of nature. It is meant not as a description of our own ingenuity as discoverers but as a comment on the resourcefulness of natural order; in the sense not so much of adaptability as of largesse and prodigality. Organisms have a life and an order of their own that scientists can only begin to fathom. "Misrepresented, not appreciated, . . . [they] are beyond our wildest expectations. . . . They do everything we [can think of], they do it better, more efficiently, more marvelously." In comparison with the ingenuity of nature, our scientific intelligence seems pallid. It follows as a matter of course that "trying to make everything fit into set dogma won't work. . . . There's no such thing as a central dogma into which everything will fit."

In the context of McClintock's views of nature, attitudes about research that would otherwise sound romantic fall into logical place. The need to "listen to the material" follows from her sense of the order of things. Precisely because the complexity of nature exceeds our own imaginative possibilities, it becomes essential to "let the experiment tell you what to do." Her major criticism of contemporary research is based on what she sees as inadequate humility. She feels that "much of the work done is done because one wants to impose an answer on it—they have the answer ready, and they [know what] they want the material to tell them, so anything it doesn't tell them, they don't really recognize as there, or they think it's a mistake and throw it out. . . . If you'd only just let the material tell you."

Respect for complexity thus demands from observers of nature the same special attention to the exceptional case that McClintock's own example as a scientist demands from observers of science: "If the material tells you, 'It may be this,' allow that. Don't turn it aside and call it an exception, an aberration, a contaminant. . . . That's what's happened all the way along the line with so many good clues."

2. All quotations from Barbara McClintock are taken from private interviews conducted between September 24, 1978, and February 25, 1979; most of them appear in Keller 1983.

Indeed, respect for individual difference lies at the very heart of McClintock's scientific passion. "The important thing is to develop the capacity to see one kernel [of maize] that is different, and make that understandable," she says. "If [something] doesn't fit, there's a reason, and you find out what it is." The prevailing focus on classes and numbers, McClintock believes, encourages researchers to overlook difference, to "call it an exception, an aberration, a contaminant." The consequences of this seem to her very costly. "Right and left," she says, they miss "what is going on."

She is, in fact, here describing the history of her own research. Her work on transposition in fact began with the observation of an aberrant pattern of pigmentation on a few kernels of a single corn plant. And her commitment to the significance of this singular pattern sustained her through six years of solitary and arduous investigation—all aimed at making the difference she saw understandable.

Making difference understandable does not mean making it disappear. In McClintock's world view, an understanding of nature can come to rest with difference. "Exceptions" are not there to "prove the rule"; they have meaning in and of themselves. In this respect, difference constitutes a principle for ordering the world radically unlike the principle of division of dichotomization (subject–object, mind–matter, feeling–reason, disorder–law). Whereas these oppositions are directed toward a cosmic unity typically excluding or devouring one of the pair, toward a unified, all-encompassing law, respect for difference remains content with multiplicity as an end in itself.

And just as the terminus of knowledge implied by difference can be distinguished from that implied by division, so the starting point of knowledge can also be distinguished. Above all, difference, in this world view, does not posit division as an epistemological prerequisite—it does not imply the necessity of hard and fast divisions in nature, or in mind, or in the relation between mind and nature. Division severs connection and imposes distance; the recognition of difference provides a starting point for relatedness. It serves both as a clue to new modes of connectedness in nature, and as an invitation to engagement with nature. For McClintock, certainly, respect for difference serves both these functions. Seeing something that does not appear to fit is, to her, a challenge to find the larger multidimensional pattern into which it does fit. Anomalous kernels of corn were evidence not of disorder or lawlessness, but of a larger system of order, one that cannot be reduced to a single law.

Difference thus invites a form of engagement and understanding that allows for the preservation of the individual. The integrity of each kernel (or chromosome or plant) survives all our own pattern-making attempts; the order of nature transcends our capacities for ordering. And this transcendence is manifested in the enduring uniqueness of each organism: "No two plants are exactly alike. They're all different, and as a consequence, you have to know that difference," she explains. "I start with the seedling, and I don't want to leave it. I don't feel I really know the story if I don't watch the plant all the way along. So I know every plant in the field. I know them intimately, and I find it a great pleasure to know them." From days, weeks, and years of patient observation comes what looks like privileged insight: "When I see things, I can interpret them right away." As one colleague described it, the result is an apparent ability to write the "autobiography" of every plant she works with.

McClintock is not here speaking of relations to other humans, but the parallels are nonetheless compelling. In the relationship she describes with plants, as in human relations, respect for difference constitutes a claim not only on our interest but on our capacity for empathy—in short on the highest form of love: love that allows for intimacy without the annihilation of difference. I use the word *love* neither loosely nor sentimentally, but out of fidelity to the language McClintock herself uses to describe a form of attention, indeed a form of thought. Her vocabulary is consistently a vocabulary of affection, of kinship, of empathy. Even with puzzles, she explains, "The thing was dear to you for a period of time, you really had an affection for it. Then after a while, it disappears and it doesn't bother you. But for a short time you feel strongly attached to that little toy." The crucial point for us is that McClintock can risk the suspension of boundaries between subject and object without jeopardy to science precisely because, to her, science is not premised on that division. Indeed, the intimacy she experiences with the objects she studies—intimacy born of a lifetime of cultivated attentiveness—is a wellspring of her powers as a scientist.

The most vivid illustration of this process comes from her own account of a breakthrough in one particularly recalcitrant piece of cytological analysis. She describes the state of mind accompanying the crucial shift in orientation that enabled her to identify chromosomes she had earlier not been able to distinguish: "I found that the more I worked with them, the bigger and bigger [the chromosomes] got, and when I was really working with them I wasn't outside, I was down there. I was part of the system. I was right down there with them, and everything got big. I even was able to see the internal parts of the chromosomes—actually everything was there. It surprised me because I actually felt as if I was right down there and these were my friends. . . . As you look at these things, they become part of you. And you forget yourself."

Cognition and Perception

In this world of difference, division is relinquished without generating chaos. Self and other, mind and nature survive not in mutual alienation, or in symbiotic fusion, but in structural integrity. The "feeling for the organism" that McClintock upholds as the sine qua non of good research need not be read as "participation mystique"; it is a mode of access—honored by time and human experience if not by prevailing conventions in science—to the reliable knowledge of the world around us that all scientists seek. It is a form of attention strongly reminiscent of the concept of "focal attention" developed by Ernest Schachtel to designate "man's [sic] capacity to center his attention on an object fully, so that he can perceive or understand it from many sides, as fully as possible" (p. 251). In Schachtel's language, "focal attention" is the principal tool that, in conjunction with our natural interest in objects per se, enables us to progress from mere wishing and wanting to thinking and knowing—that equips us for the fullest possible knowledge of reality in its own terms. Such "object-centered" perception (see chap. 6) presupposes "a temporary eclipse of all the perceiver's egocentric thoughts and strivings, of all preoccupation with self and self-esteem, and a full turning towards the object, . . . [which, in turn] leads not to a loss of self, but to a heightened feeling of aliveness" (p. 181). Object-centered perception, Schachtel goes on to argue, is in the service of a love "which wants to affirm others in their total and unique being . . . [which affirms objects as] "part of the same world of which man is a part" (p. 226). It requires

an experiential realization of the kinship between oneself
and the other . . . a realization [that] is made difficult by
fear and by arrogance—by fear because then the need to
protect oneself by flight, appeasement, or attack gets in the
way; by arrogance because then the other is no longer experienced as akin, but as inferior to oneself. (p. 227)

The difference between Schachtel and McClintock is that what
Schachtel grants to the poet's perceptual style in contrast to that of
the scientist, McClintock claims equally for science. She enlists a
"feeling for the organism"—not only for living organisms but for any
object that fully claims our attention—in pursuit of the goal shared
by all scientists: reliable (that is, shareable and reproducible) knowledge of natural order.

This difference is a direct reflection of the limitations of Schachtel's picture of science. It is drawn not from observation of scientists
like McClintock but only from the more stereotypic scientist, who
"looks at the object with one or more hypotheses . . . in mind and
thus 'uses' the object to corroborate or disprove a hypothesis, but
does not encounter the object as such, in its own fullness." For
Schachtel,

modern natural science has as its main goal prediction, i.e.
the power to manipulate objects in such a way that certain
predicted events will happen. . . . Hence, the scientist usually will tend to perceive the object merely from the perspective of [this] power. . . . That is to say that his view of
the object will be determined by the ends which he pursues
in his experimentation. . . . He may achieve a great deal in
this way and add important data to our knowledge, but to
the extent to which he remains within the framework of this
perspective he will not perceive the object in its own right.
(1959, p. 171)

To McClintock, science has a different goal: not prediction per se,
but understanding; not the power to manipulate, but empowerment—the kind of power that results from an understanding of the
world around us, that simultaneously reflects and affirms our connection to that world.

What Counts as Knowledge

At the root of this difference between McClintock and the stereotypic scientist lies that unexamined starting point of science: the naming of nature. Underlying every discussion of science, as well as every scientific discussion, there exists a larger assumption about the nature of the universe in which that discussion takes place. The power of this unseen ground is to be found not in its influence on any particular argument in science but in its framing of the very terms of argument—in its definition of the tacit aims and goals of science. As I noted in the introduction to this section, scientists may spend fruitful careers, building theories of nature that are astonishingly successful in their predictive power, without ever feeling the need to reflect on these fundamental philosophical issues. Yet if we want to ask questions about that success, about the value of alternative scientific descriptions of nature, even about the possibility of alternative criteria of success, we can do so only by examining those most basic assumptions that are normally not addressed.

We have to remind ourselves that, although all scientists share a common ambition for knowledge, it does not follow that what counts as knowledge is commonly agreed upon. The history of science reveals a wide diversity of questions asked, explanations sought, and methodologies employed in this common quest for knowledge of the natural world; this diversity is in turn reflected in the kinds of knowledge acquired, and indeed in what counts as knowledge. To a large degree, both the kinds of questions one asks and the explanations that one finds satisfying depend on one's a priori relation to the objects of study. In particular, I am suggesting that questions asked about objects with which one feels kinship are likely to differ from questions asked about objects one sees as unalterably alien. Similarly, explanations that satisfy us about a natural world that is seen as "blind, simple and dumb," ontologically inferior, may seem less self-evidently satisfying for a natural world seen as complex and, itself, resourceful. I suggest that individual and communal conceptions of nature need to be examined for their role in the history of science, not as causal determinants but as frameworks upon which all scientific programs are developed. More specifically, I am claiming that the difference between McClintock's conception of nature and that prevailing in the community around her is an essential key to our understanding of the history of her life and work.

It provides, for example, the context for examining the differences between McClintock's interests *as a geneticist* and what has historically been the defining focus of both classical and molecular genetics—differences crucial to the particular route her research took. To most geneticists, the problem of inheritance is solved by knowing the mechanism and structure of genes. To McClintock, however, as to many other biologists, mechanism and structure have never been adequate answers to the question "How do genes work?" Her focus was elsewhere: on function and organization. To her, an adequate understanding would, by definition, have to include an account of how they function in relation to the rest of the cell, and of course, to the organism as a whole.

In her language, the cell itself is an organism. Indeed, "Every component of the organism is as much an organism as every other part." When she says, therefore, that "one cannot consider the [gene] as such as being all important—more important is the overall organism," she means the genome as a whole, the cell, the ensemble of cells, the organism itself. Genes are neither "beads on a string" nor functionally disjoint pieces of DNA. They are organized functional units, whose very function is defined by their position in the organization as a whole. As she says, genes function "only with respect to the environment in which [they are] found."

Interests in function and in organization are historically and conceptually related to each other. By tradition, both are primary preoccupations of developmental biology, and McClintock's own interest in development followed from and supported these interests. By the same tradition, genetics and developmental biology have been two separate subjects. But for a geneticist for whom the answer to the question of how genes work must include function and organization, the problem of heredity becomes inseparable from the problem of development. The division that most geneticists felt they had to live with (happily or not) McClintock could not accept. To her, development, as the coordination of function, was an integral part of genetics.

McClintock's views today are clearly fed by her work on transposition. But her work on transposition was itself fed by these interests. Her own account (see Keller 1983, pp. 115–17) of how she came to this work and of how she followed the clues she saw vividly illustrates the ways in which her interests in function and organization—and in development—focused her attention on the patterns she saw and framed the questions she asked about the significance of these patterns. I suggest that they also defined the terms that a satisfying explanation had to meet.

Such an explanation had to account not so much for how transposition occurred, as for why it occurred. The patterns she saw indicated a programmatic disruption in normal developmental function. When she succeeded in linking this disruption to the location (and change in location) of particular genetic elements, that very link was what captured her interest. (She knew she was "on to something important.") The fact that transposition occurred—the fact that genetic sequences are not fixed—was of course interesting too, but only secondarily so. To her, the paramount interest lay in the meaning of its occurrence, in the clue that transposition provided for the relation between genetics and development. Necessarily, a satisfying account of this relation would have to take due note of the complexity of the regulation process.

Transposition and the Central Dogma

Just two years after McClintock's first public presentation of her work on transposition came the culminating event in the long search for the mechanism of inheritance. Watson and Crick's discovery of the structure of DNA enabled them to provide a compelling account of the essential genetic functions of replication and instruction. According to their account, the vital information of the cell is encoded in the DNA. From there it is copied onto the RNA, which, in turn, is used as a blueprint for the production of the proteins responsible for genetic traits. In the picture that emerged—DNA to RNA to protein (which Crick himself dubbed the "central dogma")—the DNA is posited as the central actor in the cell, the executive governor of cellular organization, itself remaining impervious to influence from the subordinate agents to which it dictates. Several years later, Watson and Crick's original model was emended by Jacques Monod and François Jacob to allow for environmental control of the rates of protein synthesis. But even with this modification, the essential autonomy of DNA remained unchallenged: information flowed one way, always from, and never to, the DNA.

Throughout the 1950s and 1960s, the successes of molecular

genetics were dramatic. By the end of the 1960s, it was possible to say (as Jacques Monod did say), "The Secret of Life? But this is in large part known—in principle, if not in details" (quoted in Judson 1979, p. 216). A set of values and interests wholly different from McClintock's seemed to have been vindicated. The intricacies, and difficulties, of corn genetics held little fascination in comparison with the quick returns from research on the vastly simpler and seemingly more straightforward bacterium and bacteriophage. As a result, communication between McClintock and her colleagues grew steadily more difficult; fewer and fewer biologists had the expertise required even to begin to understand her results.

McClintock of course shared in the general excitement of this period, but she did not share in the general enthusiasm for the central dogma. The same model that seemed so immediately and overwhelmingly satisfying to so many of her colleagues did not satisfy her. Although duly impressed by its explanatory power, she remained at the same time acutely aware of what it did not explain. It neither addressed the questions that were of primary interest to her—bearing on the relation between genetics and development—nor began to take into account the complexity of genetic organization that she had always assumed, and that was now revealed to her by her work on transposition.

McClintock locates the critical flaw of the central dogma in its presumption: it claimed to explain too much. Baldly put, what was true of *E. coli* (the bacterium most commonly studied) was *not* true of the elephant, as Monod (and others) would have had it (Judson 1979, p. 613). Precisely because higher organisms are multicellular, she argued, they necessarily require a different kind of economy. The central dogma was without question inordinately successful as well as scientifically productive. Yet the fact that it ultimately proved inadequate even to the dynamics of *E. coli* suggests that its trouble lay deeper than just a too hasty generalization from the simple to the complex; its presumptuousness, I suggest, was built into its form of explanation.

The central dogma is a good example of what I have earlier called (following Nanney 1957) master-molecule theories (Keller 1982). In locating the seat of genetic control in a single molecule, it posits a structure of genetic organization that is essentially hierarchical, often illustrated in textbooks by organizational charts like those of corporate structures. In this model, genetic stability is ensured by the unidirectionality of information flow, much as political and social stability is assumed in many quarters to require the unidirectional exercise of authority.

To McClintock, transposition provided evidence that genetic organization is necessarily more complex, and in fact more globally interdependent, than such a model assumes. It showed that the DNA itself is subject to rearrangement and, by implication, to reprogramming. Although she did not make the suggestion explicit, the hidden heresy of her argument lay in the inference that such reorganization could be induced by signals external to the DNA—from the cell, the organism, even from the environment.

For more than fifty years, modern biologists had labored heroically to purge biological thought of the last vestiges of teleology, particularly as they surfaced in Lamarckian notions of adaptive evolution. But even though McClintock is not a Lamarckian, she sees in transposition a mechanism enabling genetic structures to respond to the needs of the organism. Since needs are relative to the environmental context and hence subject to change, transposition, by implication, indirectly allows for the possibility of environmentally induced and genetically transmitted change. To her, such a possibility is not heresy—it is not even surprising. On the contrary, it is in direct accord with her belief in the resourcefulness of natural order. Because she has no investment in the passivity of nature, the possibility of internally generated order does not, to her, threaten the foundations of science. The capacity of organisms to reprogram their own DNA implies neither vitalism, magic, nor a countermanding will. It merely confirms the existence of forms of order more complex than we have, at least thus far, been able to account for.

The renewed interest in McClintock's work today is a direct consequence of developments (beginning in the early 1970s) in the very research programs that had seemed so philosophically opposed to her position; genetic mobility was rediscovered within molecular biology itself. That this was so was crucial, perhaps even necessary, to establishing the legitimacy of McClintock's early work, precisely because the weight of scientific authority has now come to reside in molecular biology. As a by-product, this legitimization also lends McClintock's views of science and attitudes toward research somewhat more credibility among professional biologists. To observers of science, this same historical sequence serves as a sharp reminder that the languages of science, however self-contained they seem, are not closed. McClintock's

> eventual vindication demonstrates the capacity of science to overcome its own characteristic kinds of myopia, reminding us that its limitations do not reinforce themselves indefinitely. Their own methodology allows, even obliges, scientists to continually reencounter phenomena even their best theories cannot accommodate. Or—to look at it from the other side—however severely communication between science and nature may be impeded by the preconceptions of a particular time, some channels always remain open; and, through them, nature finds ways of reasserting itself. (Keller 1983, p. 197)

In this sense, the McClintock story is a happy one.

It is important, however, not to overestimate the degree of rapprochement that has taken place. McClintock has been abundantly vindicated: transposition is acknowledged, higher organisms and development have once again captured the interest of biologists, and almost everyone agrees that genetic organization is manifestly more complex than had previously been thought. But not everyone shares her conviction that we are in the midst of a revolution that "will reorganize the way we look at things, the way we do research." Many researchers remain confident that the phenomenon of transposition can somehow be incorporated, even if they do not yet see how, into an improved version of the central dogma. Their attachment to this faith is telling. Behind the continuing skepticism about McClintock's interpretation of the role of transposition in development and evolution, there remains a major gap between her underlying interests and commitments and those of most of her colleagues.

The Issue of Gender

How much of this enduring difference reflects the fact that McClintock is a woman in a field still dominated by men? To what extent are her views indicative of a vision of "what will happen to science," as Erik Erikson asked in 1964 (1965, p. 243), "if and when women are truly represented in it—not by a few glorious exceptions, but in the rank and file of the scientific elite?"

On the face of it, it would be tempting indeed to call Mc-Clintock's vision of science "a feminist science." Its emphasis on intuition, on feeling, on connection and relatedness, all seem to confirm our most familiar stereotypes of women. And to the extent that they do, we might expect that the sheer presence of more women in science would shift the balance of community sentiment and lead to the endorsement of that vision. However, there are both general and particular reasons that argue strongly against this simple view.

The general argument is essentially the same as that which I made against the notion of "a different science," in the introduction to part 3. To the extent that science is defined by its past and present practitioners, anyone who aspires to membership in that community must conform to its existing code. As a consequence, the inclusion of new members, even from a radically different culture, cannot induce immediate or direct change. To be a successful scientist, one must first be adequately socialized. For this reason, it is unreasonable to expect a sharp differentiation between women scientists and their male colleagues, and indeed, most women scientists would be appalled by such a suggestion.

McClintock is in this sense no exception. She would disclaim any analysis of her work as a woman's work, as well as any suggestion that her views represent a woman's perspective. To her, science is not a matter of gender, either male or female; it is, on the contrary, a place where (ideally at least) "the matter of gender drops away." Furthermore, her very commitment to science is of a piece with her lifelong wish to transcend gender altogether. Indeed, her adamant rejection of female stereotypes seems to have been a prerequisite for her becoming a scientist at all. (See Keller 1983, chaps. 2 and 3.) In her own image of herself, she is a maverick in all respects—as a woman, as a scientist, even as a woman scientist.

Finally, I want to reemphasize that it would be not only misleading but actually contradictory to suggest that McClintock's views of science were shared by none of her colleagues. Had that been so, she could not have had even marginal status as a scientist. It is essential to understand that, in practice, the scientific tradition is far more pluralistic than any particular description of it suggests, and certainly more pluralistic than its dominant ideology. For McClintock to be recognized as a scientist, the positions that she represents, however unrepresentative, had to be, and were, identifiable as belonging somewhere within that tradition.

But although McClintock is not a total outsider to science, she is equally clearly not an insider. And however atypical she is as a woman, what she is *not* is a man. Between these two facts lies a crucial connection—a connection signaled by the recognition that, as McClintock herself admits, the matter of gender never does drop away.

I suggest that the radical core of McClintock's stance can be located right here: Because she is not a man, in a world of men, her commitment to a gender-free science has been binding; because concepts of gender have so deeply influenced the basic categories of science, that commitment has been transformative. In short, the relevance of McClintock's gender in this story is to be found not in its role in her personal socialization but precisely in the role of gender in the construction of science.

Of course, not all scientists have embraced the conception of science as one of "putting nature on the rack and torturing the answers out of her." Nor have all men embraced a conception of masculinity that demands cool detachment and domination. Nor even have all scientists been men. But most have. And however variable the attitudes of individual male scientists toward science and toward masculinity, the metaphor of a marriage between mind and nature necessarily does not look the same to them as it does to women. And this is the point.

In a science constructed around the naming of object (nature) as female and the parallel naming of subject (mind) as male, any scientist who happens to be a woman is confronted with an a priori contradiction in terms. This poses a critical problem of identity: any scientist who is not a man walks a path bounded on one side by inauthenticity and on the other by subversion. Just as surely as inauthenticity is the cost a woman suffers by joining men in misogynist jokes, so it is, equally, the cost suffered by a woman who identifies with an image of the scientist modeled on the patriarchal husband. Only if she undergoes a radical disidentification from self can she share masculine pleasure in mastering a nature cast in the image of

woman as passive, inert, and blind. Her alternative is to attempt a
radical redefinition of terms. Nature must be renamed as not female,
or, at least, as not an alienated object. By the same token, the mind,
if the female scientist is to have one, must be renamed as not necessarily male, and accordingly recast with a more inclusive subjectivity. This is not to say that the male scientist cannot claim similar
redefinition (certainly many have done so) but, by contrast to the
woman scientist, his identity does not require it.

For McClintock, given her particular commitments to personal
integrity, to be a scientist, and not a man, with a nonetheless intact
identity, meant that she had to insist on a different meaning of mind,
of nature, and of the relation between them. Her need to define for
herself the relation between subject and object, even the very terms
themselves, came not from a feminist consciousness, or even from
a female consciousness. It came from her insistence on her right to
be a scientist—from her determination to claim science as a human
rather than a male endeavor. For such a claim, difference makes
sense of the world in ways that division cannot. It allows for the
kinship that she feels with other scientists, without at the same time
obligating her to share all their assumptions.

Looked at in this way, McClintock's stance is, finally, a far more
radical one than that implied in Erikson's question. It implies that
what could happen to science "when women are truly represented
in it" is not simply, or even, "the addition, to the male kind of
creative vision, of women's vision" (p. 243), but, I suggest, a thor-
oughgoing transformation of the very possibilities of creative vision,
for everyone. It implies that the kind of change we might hope for
is not a direct or readily apparent one but rather an indirect and
subterranean one. A first step toward such a transformation would
be the undermining of the commitment of scientists to the masculinity of their profession that would be an inevitable concomitant of
the participation of large numbers of women.

However, we need to remember that, as long as success in science does not require self-reflection, the undermining of masculinist
or other ideological commitments is not a sufficient guarantee of
change. But nature itself is an ally that can be relied upon to provide
the impetus for real change: nature's responses recurrently invite
reexamination of the terms in which our understanding of science is

constructed. Paying attention to those responses—"listening to the material"—may help us to reconstruct our understanding of science in terms born out of the diverse spectrum of human experience rather than out of the narrow spectrum that our culture has labeled masculine.

Epilogue

Over the past decade the internal logic of feminist criticism in the natural sciences, like that of feminist scholarship in general, has shifted it—inexorably, in retrospect—along a spectrum from liberal to radical (see Keller 1982). Early feminist work focused almost entirely on the absence of women in science, and on the barriers responsible for that absence. Early scholarship was directly coupled with the political demand for equity. Soon, attention naturally turned to the scientific consequences of the historical underrepresentation of women in the sciences. Scholars began to ask how that underrepresentation has skewed choices of problems, and then, how inadvertent bias has crept into the design of experiments and the interpretation of data, especially in the human and animal (that is, "softer") sciences. Insofar as these criticisms could be simply met— by imposing existing scientific standards more vigilantly—they remain in what I call the liberal domain. Bias, in this view (androcentric or otherwise), is a result merely of insufficient rigor, a failing to which the "harder" sciences would presumably not be prone. But how, one begins to ask, are "hard" and "soft" defined? Following the pattern in other disciplines, feminist scholars inevitably began to question the gender neutrality of the very criteria defining "scientific" (see, for example, Keller 1978, Harding 1979 and 1982, and Merchant 1980): objectivity itself came under suspicion as an androcentric goal. Some authors concluded that perhaps, after all, science *is* a masculine project.

The essays in this book belong to the radical end of such a spectrum. But one strand of the radical feminist critique goes on from the hypothesis of deep-rooted androcentrism in science either to reject science altogether, or to demand that it be replaced—in toto—by a radically different science. Because I am a scientist, the first of these moves is, for me, simply untenable. It also seems suicidal: as I wrote elsewhere, "By rejecting objectivity as a masculine ideal, it simultaneously lends its voice to an enemy chorus and dooms women to residing outside of the realpolitik modern culture; it exacerbates the very problem it wishes to solve" (Keller 1982, p. 593).

The second proposal, perhaps also because I am a scientist, seems to me equally problematic. The assumption that science *can* be replaced, de novo, reflects a view of science as pure social product, owing obedience to moral and political pressure from without. In this extreme relativism, science dissolves into ideology; any emancipatory function of modern science is negated, and the arbitration of truth recedes into the political domain. My view of science—and of the possibilities of at least a partial sorting of cognitive from ideological—is more optimistic. And accordingly, the aim of these essays is more exacting: it is the reclamation, from within science, of science as a human instead of a masculine project, and the renunciation of the division of emotional and intellectual labor that maintains science as a male preserve.

All the essays are, in one way or another, preoccupied with androcentric bias in prevailing definitions of science; their aim throughout is the transcendence of that bias. I have used a feminist analysis to help clarify part of the substructure of science in order to preserve the things that science has taught us, in order to be more objective.

My vision of a gender-free science is not a juxtaposition or complementarity of male and female perspectives, nor is it the substitution of one form of parochiality for another. Rather, it is premised on a transformation of the very categories of male and female, and correspondingly, of mind and nature.

At the same time, I take seriously the lessons in the philosophy of difference I read from McClintock's example. That philosophy has taught me to seek a science named not by gender, or even by androgyny, but by many different kinds of naming. A healthy science is one that allows for the productive survival of diverse conceptions of mind and nature, and of correspondingly diverse strategies. In my vision of science, it is not the taming of nature that is sought, but the taming of hegemony.

To know the history of science is to recognize the mortality of any claim to universal truth. Every past vision of scientific truth, every model of natural phenomena, has proved in time to be more limited than its adherents claimed. The survival of productive difference in science requires that we put all claims for intellectual hegemony in their proper place—that we understand that such claims are, by their very nature, political rather than scientific.

Bibliography

Ainsworth, Mary 1969. Object Relations, Dependency and Attachment. *Child Development* 49, pp. 969–1025.

Allen, Sally, and Hubbs, Joanna 1980. Outrunning Atalanta: Feminine Destiny in Alchemical Transmutation. *Signs* 6, pp. 210–29.

Anderson, F. H., ed. 1960. *Francis Bacon: The New Organon and Related Writings.* Indianapolis: Bobbs Merrill.

Baines, Barbara J., ed. 1978. *Three Pamphlets on the Jacobean Antifeminist Controversy.* Delmar, N.Y.: Scholars' Facsimiles and Reprints.

Balbus, Isaac 1981. *Marxism and Domination.* Princeton: Princeton University Press.

Bataille, Georges 1977. *Death and Sensuality.* New York: Arno Press.

Bellak, Leopold, and Antell, Maxine 1974. An Intercultural Study of Aggressive Behavior on Children's Playgrounds. *American Journal of Orthopsychiatry* 44, no. 4, pp. 503–11.

Benderly, Beryl Lieff 1982. Rape Free or Rape Prone. *Science 82* October, pp. 40–43.

Benjamin, Jessica 1980. The Bonds of Love: Rational Violence and Erotic Domination. *Feminist Studies* 6, no. 1, pp. 144–74.

Benjamin, Jessica 1982. The Oedipal Riddle: Authority, Autonomy and the New Narcissism. In *The Problem of Authority in America,* ed. John P. Diggens and Mark E. Kahn. Philadelphia: Temple University Press.

Bonner, J. T. et al. 1969. Acrasin, Acrasinase, and the Sensitivity to Acrasin in *Dictyostelium Discoideum. Developmental Biology* 20, pp. 72–87.

Bowlby, John 1969. *Attachment and Loss.* 3 vols. London: Hogarth Press.

Boyle, Robert 1690. A Free Inquiry into the Vulgar Notion of Nature. Reprinted in *Philosophical Works,* ed. Peter Shaw. London, 1738.

Charleton, Walter 1659. *The Ephesian Matron.* London. William Andrews Clark Memorial Library, Univ. of California, 1975.

Chodorow, Nancy 1974. Family Structure and Feminine Personality. In *Woman, Culture and Society,* ed. M. Z. Rosaldo and L. Lamphere. Stanford: Stanford University Press.

Chodorow, Nancy 1978. *The Reproduction of Mothering: Psychoanalysis and the Sociology of Gender.* Berkeley: University of California Press.

BIBLIOGRAPHY

Chodorow, Nancy 1979. Feminism and Difference: Gender, Relation and Difference in Psychoanalytic Perspective. *Socialist Review* 46.

Chodorow, Nancy, and Contratto, Susan 1982. The Fantasy of the Perfect Mother. In *Rethinking the Family: Some Feminist Questions*, ed. Barrie Thorne with Marilyn Yalom. New York: Longman.

Cixous, Hélène 1975. Sorties. In *New French Feminisms*, ed. Elaine Marks and Isabelle de Courtivron. New York: Schocken, 1981.

Clark, Alice 1919. *Working Life of Women in the Seventeenth Century.* London. Reprints of Economic Classics. New York, 1968.

Cohen, M., and Hagan, P. 1981. Diffusion-Induced Morphogenesis in *Dictyostelium. Journal of Theoretical Biology* 93, pp. 881–908.

Cohen, M., and Robertson, A. 1971a. Chemotaxis and the Early Stages of Aggregation in Cellular Slime Molds. *Journal of Theoretical Biology* 31, pp. 119–30.

Cohen, M., and Robertson, A. 1971b. Wave Propagation in the Early Stages of Aggregation in Cellular Slime Molds. *Journal of Theoretical Biology* 31, pp. 101–18.

Collingwood, R. G. 1945. *The Idea of Nature.* Reprinted by Oxford University Press, New York, 1981.

Contratto, Susan 1983. Father Presence in Women's Psychological Development. To be published in *Studies in Psychoanalytic Sociology*, ed. J. Rabow, M. Goldman, and G. Platt. Melbourne, Fla.: Krieger & Co.

Davis, Natalie 1975. *Society and Culture in Early Modern France.* Stanford: Stanford University Press.

Davis, Natalie 1977. Men, Women, and Violence: Some Reflections on Equality. *Smith Alumnae Quarterly* April, pp. 12–15.

de Beauvoir, Simone 1970. *The Second Sex.* New York: Alfred A. Knopf.

Debus, Allen G., ed. 1972. *Science, Medicine and Society in the Renaissance.* New York: Science, History Publications.

Debus, Allen G. 1978. *Man and Nature in the Renaissance.* New York and Cambridge: Cambridge University Press.

Dinnerstein, Dorothy 1976. *The Mermaid and the Minotaur.* New York: Harper & Row.

Dobbs, Betty Jo Teeter 1975. *The Foundations of Newton's Alchemy or "The Hunting of the Greene Lyon."* Cambridge: Cambridge University Press.

Dover, K. J. 1978. *Greek Homosexuality.* New York: Vintage Books, 1980.

Easlea, Brian 1980. *Witch Hunting, Magic and the New Philosophy.* Brighton: Harvester Press.

Ehrenreich, Barbara, and English, Deirdre 1978. *For Her Own Good: 150 Years of the Experts' Advice to Women.* Garden City, N.Y.: Anchor Press, Doubleday.

Eisenstein, Hester 1979. Workshop 12. *The Second Sex: Thirty Years Later.* New York, Sept. 28.

Elias, Norbert 1939. *The History of Manners.* New York: Pantheon 1978. Originally published as *Uber den Prozess der Zivilisation,* 1939. Switzerland: Haus zum Falken.

Ellman, Mary 1968. *Thinking About Women.* New York: Harcourt, Brace Jovanovich.

Erikson, Erik H. 1965. Concluding Remarks. In *Women in the Scientific Professions,* ed. J. Mattfeld and C. van Aiken, Cambridge: MIT Press.

Erikson, Erik H. 1968. *Identity: Youth and Crisis.* New York: W. W. Norton.

Fairbairn, W. R. D. 1952. *An Object-Relations Theory of the Personality.* New York: Basic Books.

Farrington, Benjamin 1951. Temporis Partus Masculus: An Untranslated Writing of Francis Bacon. *Centaurus,* 1.

Farrington, Benjamin 1964. *The Philosophy of Francis Bacon.* Chicago: Phoenix.

Feynman, Richard 1963. *The Feynman Lectures on Physics,* ed. Richard Feynman et al., Reading, Mass.: Addison-Wesley.

Finkelstein, David 1964. *Transactions of the N.Y. Academy* 6, p. 21.

Flax, Jane 1978. The Conflict between Nurturance and Autonomy in Mother-Daughter Relationships and Within Feminism. *Feminist Studies* 4, June, pp. 171–89.

Freud, Sigmund 1930. *Civilization and its Discontents.* Trans. Joan Riviere. New York: Anchor Press, Doubleday.

Freud, Sigmund 1940. *Outline of Psychoanalysis.* Trans. James Strachey. New York: Norton 1949.

Freud, Sigmund 1949. A Special Type of Object-Choice. *Collected Papers,* ed. J. Riviere, 5 vols. London: Hogarth Press and the Institute of Psycho-Analysis.

Freud, Sigmund 1957. *The Ego and the Id.* In *A General Selection From the Works of Sigmund Freud,* ed. J. Rickman. New York: Doubleday.

Fromm, Erich 1973. *The Anatomy of Human Destructiveness.* New York: Holt, Rinehart and Winston.

Gay, Peter 1984. *The Education of the Senses.* New Haven: Yale University Press.

Gilligan, Carol 1982. *In a Different Voice: Psychological Theory and Women's Development.* Cambridge: Harvard University Press.

Glanvill, Joseph 1661. *The Vanity of Dogmatizing.* London. Reprinted by Facsimile Text Society, 1931. New York: Columbia University Press.

Glanvill, Joseph 1668. *A Blow at Modern Sadducism.* London.

Glanvill, Joseph 1689. *Sadducismus Triumphatus: or, Full and Plain Evi-*

dence Concerning Witches and Apparitions. London. Reprinted by Scholars' Facsimiles and Reprints, Gainesville, Fla., 1966.

Golden, Mark 1981. *Aspects of Childhood in Classical Athens.* University of Toronto, unpublished thesis.

Goodfield, June 1981. *An Imagined World.* New York: Harper & Row.

Greenson, R. 1968. Disidentifying from Mother: Its Special Importance for the Boy. *Explorations in Psychoanalysis.* New York: International Universities Press, 1978.

Guntrip, Harry 1961. *Personality Structure and Human Interaction.* New York: International Universities Press.

Hagan, P. 1981. Target Patterns in Reaction-Diffusion Systems. *Advances in Applied Mathematics* 2, pp. 400–16.

Halperin, David M. 1983. Plato and Erotic Reciprocity. Unpublished manuscript.

Hanson, Norwood 1959. *Patterns of Discovery.* Cambridge: Cambridge University Press.

Harding, Sandra 1979. "Is Science Objective?" presented at the annual meeting of the American Association for the Advancement of Science, Houston, Texas, January 6, 1979.

Harding, Sandra 1982. Is Gender a Variable in Conceptions of Rationality? *Dialectica* 36, pp. 225–42.

Hartsock, Nancy 1983. *Money, Sex and Power.* New York: Longman.

Hill, Christopher 1975. *The World Turned Upside Down: Radical Ideas During the English Revolution.* London: Penguin.

Holton, Gerald 1974. On Being Caught Between Dionysians and Apollonians. *Daedalus,* Summer 1974, pp. 65–81.

Horney, Karen 1926. The Flight from Womanhood. In *Women and Analysis,* ed. J. Strouse. New York: Dell, 1975.

Hudson, L. 1972. *The Cult of the Fact.* New York: Harper & Row.

Jacob, J. R. 1977. *Robert Boyle and the English Revolution.* New York: B. Franklin.

Jacob, Margaret 1976. *The Newtonians and the English Revolution, 1689–1728.* Ithaca: Cornell University Press.

Jacob, Margaret 1981. *The Radical Enlightenment: Pantheists, Freemen and Republicans.* London: Allen & Unwin.

Jacobi, Jolandt, ed. 1951. *Paracelsus: Selected Writings.* Princeton: Princeton University Press.

Jobe, Thomas Harmon 1981. The Devil in Restoration Science: The Glanvill–Webster Debate. *ISIS* 72, pp. 343–56.

Judson, Horace 1979. *The Eighth Day of Creation: Makers of the Revolution in Biology.* New York: Simon & Schuster.

Jung, Karl 1980. *Psychology and Alchemy.* Princeton: Bollingen Press, 1980.

Keller, Evelyn Fox 1974. Women in Science: A Social Analysis. *Harvard Magazine* October, pp. 14–19.

Keller, Evelyn Fox 1978. Gender and Science. *Psychoanalysis and Contemporary Thought* 1, 409–33. Reprinted as chapter 4 in the present volume.

Keller, Evelyn Fox 1982. Feminism and Science. *Signs: Journal of Women in Culture and Society* 7, no. 3, pp. 589–602.

Keller, Evelyn Fox 1983. *A Feeling for the Organism: The Life and Work of Barbara McClintock.* New York: Freeman.

Keller, Evelyn Fox, and Grontkowski, Christine R. 1983. The Mind's Eye. In *Discovering Reality*, ed. S. Harding and M. Hintikka. Dordrecht, Holland: Reidel.

Keller, Evelyn Fox, and Segel, Lee A. 1970. Initiation of Slime Mold Aggregation Viewed as an Instability. *Journal of Theoretical Biology* 26, pp. 399–415.

Kelly, Joan 1982. Early Feminist Theory and the *Querelle des Femmes.* *Signs* 8, no. 1, pp. 1–28.

Kernberg, O. 1977. Boundaries and Structure in Love Relations. *Journal of the American Psychoanalytic Association* 25, pp. 81–114.

Kohut, Heinz 1971. *The Analysis of the Self.* New York: International Universities Press.

Kohut, Heinz 1977. *The Restoration of the Self.* New York: International Universities Press.

Kopell, Nancy 1980. Patterns in Nature: The Character of Mathematical Modelling. Boston: Robert D. Klein University Lecture, Northeastern University.

Kopell, Nancy 1981. Target Pattern Solution to Reaction-Diffusion Equations in the Presence of Impurities. *Advances in Applied Mathematics* 2, pp. 389–99.

Koyré, Alexander 1968. *Newtonian Studies.* Chicago: University of Chicago Press, p. 23.

Kramer, H., and Sprenger, J. 1486. *Malleus Maleficarum.* New York: Bloom, 1970.

Kuhn, Thomas S. 1962. *The Structure of Scientific Revolutions.* Chicago: University of Chicago Press.

Lasch, Christopher 1979. *The Culture of Narcissism: American Life in an Age of Diminishing Expectations.* New York: W. W. Norton.

Leiss, William 1972. *The Domination of Nature.* Boston: Beacon Press.

Levinson, Daniel J. 1978. *The Seasons of a Man's Life.* New York: Alfred A. Knopf.

Loewald, Hans 1951. Ego and Reality. *International Journal of Psycho-Analysis* 32, pp. 10–18.

Loewald, Hans 1979. The Waning of the Oedipus Complex. *Journal of the American Psychoanalytic Association* 27, no. 4, pp. 751–75.

McClelland, D. C. 1962. On the Dynamics of Creative Physical Scientists. In *The Ecology of Human Intelligence*, ed. L. Hudson. Harmondsworth: Penguin Books.

Mack, Phyllis 1982. Women as Prophets During the English Civil War. *Feminist Studies* 8, no. 1, pp. 19–46.

MacKinnon, Catherine A. Feminism, Marxism, Method and the State: An Agenda for Theory. *Signs* 7, pp. 515–44.

Marcus, Steven 1977. *The Other Victorians: A Study of Sexuality and Pornography in Mid-Nineteenth Century England*. New York: New American Library.

Marx, Jean L. 1981. A Movable Feast in the Eukaryotic Genome. *Science* 211, p. 153.

May, Robert 1980. *Sex and Fantasy*. New York: Wideview Books, 1981. First published by W. W. Norton.

Merchant, Carolyn 1980. *The Death of Nature*. San Francisco: Harper & Row.

Miller, Jean Baker 1976. *Toward a New Psychology of Women*. Boston: Beacon Press.

Miller, Jean Baker 1983. Development of the Sense of Self in Women. Presented at the American Academy of Psychoanalysis, October.

Milner, Marion 1957. *On Not Being Able to Paint*. New York: International Universities Press.

More, Henry 1650. *Observations upon Anthroposophia Theomagica and Anima Magic Obscondita*. London, 1650.

More, Henry 1656. *Enthusiasmus triumphatus*. London.

More, Henry 1678. Postscript to letter to Jos. Glanvill, May 25, 1678. Published in Glanvill, *Saducismus Triumphatus*.

More, Henry 1712. Scholia on the Antidote against Atheism. In *A Collection of Several Philosophical Writings of Dr. Henry More*. London.

Mott, N. F. 1964. *Contemporary Physics* 5, pp. 401–18.

Nanney, David L. 1957. The Role of the Cytoplasm in Heredity. In *The Chemical Basis of Heredity*, ed. W. D. McElroy and H. B. Glass. Baltimore: Johns Hopkins University Press.

Newton, Isaac 1706. *Opticks*, 3d edition. London 1921.

Painter, T. S. 1971. Chromosomes and Genes Viewed from a Perspective of Fifty Years of Research. *Stadler Genetics Symposium* 1, p. 33.

Partridge, Eric 1969. *Shakespeare's Bawdy*. New York: E. P. Dutton.

Peres, Asher 1974. *American Journal of Physics* 42, p. 401.

Perry, Ruth 1980. *Women, Letters and the Novel*. New York: AMS Press.

Piaget, Jean 1972. *The Child's Conception of the World*. Totowa, N.J.: Littlefield, Adams.

Piaget, Jean 1973. The Affective Unconscious and the Cognitive Unconscious. *Journal of the American Psychoanalytic Association* 21, pp. 249–61.

Pine, Fred 1979. On the Pathology of the Separation-Individuation Process as Manifested in Later Clinical Work: An Attempt at Delineation. *International Journal of Psycho-Analysis* 60, pp. 225–42.

Plank, E. N., and Plank, R. 1954. Emotional Components in Arithmetic Learning as Seen Through Autobiographies. *The Psychoanalytic Study of the Child* 9. New York: International Universities Press.

Plato. *The Symposium*. Trans. Walter Hamilton. Harmondsworth: Penguin Books, 1955.

Plato. *The Republic*. Trans. H. D. P. Lee. Harmondsworth: Penguin Books, 1955.

Plato. *Phaedrus*. Trans. Walter Hamilton. Harmondsworth: Penguin Books, 1973.

Polanyi, Michael 1967. *The Tacit Dimension*. Garden City, N.Y.: Anchor Books, Doubleday.

Rattansi, P. M. 1963. Paracelsus and the Puritan Revolution. *Ambix* 11, pp. 24–32.

Rattansi, P. M. 1968. The Intellectual Origins of the Royal Society. *Notes and Records of the Royal Society of London* 23, pp. 129–43.

Robertson, J. H. 1905. *Valerius Terminus of the Interpretation of Nature*. In *The Philosophical Works of Francis Bacon*. London: Routledge & Sons.

Roe, A. 1953. *The Making of a Scientist*. New York: Dodd, Mead.

Roe, A. 1956. *The Psychology of Occupations*. New York: Wiley.

Rossi, Paolo 1968. *Francis Bacon: From Magic to Science*. Chicago: University of Chicago Press.

Rossiter, Margaret W. 1982. *Women Scientists in America*. Baltimore: Johns Hopkins University Press.

Rowbotham, Sheila 1974. *Hidden from History: Rediscovering Women in History from the 17th Century to the Present*. New York: Random House.

Ruddick, Sara 1983. Preservative Love and Military Destruction: Some Reflections on Mothering and Peace. In *Mothering: Essays in Feminist Theory*, ed. Joyce Tribilcot. Totoya, N.J.: Rowman and Allenheld.

Schachtel, Ernest 1959. *Metamorphosis*. New York: Basic Books.

Schrödinger, Erwin 1954. *Nature and the Greeks*. New York and Cambridge: Cambridge University Press.

Schrödinger, Erwin 1967. *Mind and Matter*. New York and Cambridge: Cambridge University Press.

Shaffer, B. M. 1962. The Acrasina. *Advances in Morphogenesis* 2, pp. 109–82.

Shapiro, David 1965. *Neurotic Styles*. New York: Basic Books.

Shapiro, David 1981. *Autonomy and Rigid Character*. New York: Basic Books.

Simmel, Georg 1911. The Relative and the Absolute in the Problem of the Sexes. *On Women, Sexuality, and Love*, 3d ed., 1923. Trans. Guy Oakes. New Haven: Yale University Press, 1984.

Spedding, J., Ellis, R. L., and Heath, D. D., eds. 1857–74. 14 vols. *The Works of Francis Bacon*. Reprinted 1963, Stuttgart: F. F. Verlag.

Sprat, Thomas 1667. *The History of the Royal Society of London, for the Improving of Natural Knowledge*, ed. J. I. Cope and H. W. Jones. London: Routledge, 1966.

Stern, Daniel 1977. *The First Relationship*. Cambridge: Harvard University Press.

Stern, Daniel 1983. "The Early Development of Schemas of Self, Other, and 'Self with Other.'" In *Reflections on Self Psychology*, ed. J. D. Lichtenberg and S. Kaplan. New York: International Universities Press.

Storr, Anthony 1972. *The Dynamics of Creation*. New York: Atheneum.

Thomas, Keith 1971. *Religion and the Decline of Magic*. New York: Scribner.

Thomas, Keith 1958. Women and the Civil War Sects. *Past and Present* 13, pp. 42–62.

Thomas, Keith 1959. The Double Standard. *Journal of the History of Ideas* 20, pp. 195–216.

Traweek, Sharon 1982. *Uptime, Downtime, Spacetime and Power: An Ethnographic Study of the High Energy Physics Community in Japan and the United States*. Unpublished dissertation, UCSC.

Traweek, Sharon 1984. The Consequences of the Absence of Women in Science. Lecture at MIT, March 19.

Turing, Alan M. 1952. The Chemical Basis of Morphogenesis. *Proceedings of the Royal Society of London [Biology]* 237, p. 37.

Vaughan, Thomas 1650a. *Anthroposophia Theomagica, or A discourse of the nature of man and his state after death*. In *The Works of Thomas Vaughan*, ed. Arthur E. Waite. London: Theosophical Publishing House, 1919.

Vaughan, Thomas 1650b. *Anima Magica Abscondita: Or A Discourse of the universall Spirit of Nature*. In *The Works of Thomas Vaughan*, ed. Arthur E. Waite. London: Theosophical Publishing House, 1919.

Van den Daele, Wolfgang 1977. The Social Construction of Science: Institutionalisation and Definition of Positive Science in the Latter Half of the Seventeenth Century. In *The Social Production of Scientific Knowledge*, eds. E. Mendelsohn, P. Wengart, and R. Whitley. Dordrecht, Holland: Reidel.

Vlastos, Gregory 1970. Equality and Justice in Early Greek Cosmologies. In *Studies in Presocratic Philosophy*, ed. D. J. Furley and R. E. Allen, vol. 1. London: Routledge & Kegan Paul.

Vlastos, Gregory 1981. *Platonic Studies*. Princeton: Princeton University Press.

Watson, James 1966. Growing Up in the Phage Group. In *Phage and the Origins of Molecular Biology*, ed. J. Cairns, G. Stent, and J. Watson. Cold Spring Harbor, N.Y.: Cold Spring Harbor Laboratory of Quantitative Biology.

Webster, Charles 1975. *The Great Instauration*. New York: Holmes and Meier.

Webster, John 1654. *Academiarum Examen*. London, p. 106.

Weinberg, Steven 1974. Reflections of a Working Scientist. *Daedalus* Summer, pp. 33–46.

Wigner, Eugene 1975. The Nature of Consciousness. Seminar at Vassar College, October 10.

Winfree, A. 1980. *The Geometry of Biological Time*. New York: Springer-Verlag.

Winnicott, D. W. 1971. *Playing and Reality*. New York: Basic Books.

Yates, Frances 1969. *Giordano Bruno and the Hermetic Tradition*. New York: Vintage.

Yates, Frances 1978. *The Rosicrucian Enlightenment*. Boulder: Shambhala.

NAME INDEX

Aeschylus, 22
Agrippa, Marcus Vipsanius, 43, 48
Ainsworth, Mary, 113
Allen, Sally, 53
Antell, Maxine, 104
Aristotle, 39, 45, 49
Ashmole, Elias, 46

Bacon, Francis, 7, 18, 31, 33–42,
  47, 48, 51–54, 91, 93, 115, 132
Balbus, Isaac, 111–12
Bataille, Georges, 105
Bellak, Leopold, 104
Benderly, Beryl, 114
Benjamin, Jessica, 72, 103, 105, 109
Bonner, John, 151
Bowlby, John, 113
Boyle, Robert, 11, 46, 54, 131

Casaubon, Meric, 57
Charleton, Walter, 46, 60
Chodorow, Nancy, 72, 73, 89, 101,
  106–09, 111, 113
Cixous, Hélène, 42
Clark, Alice, 63
Cohen, Marcus, 152, 155–56
Coleridge, Samuel Taylor, 158
Collingwood, R. G., 22
Contratto, Susan, 111
Crick, Francis, 169
Cudworth, Ralph, 58

Davis, Natalie, 62
de Beauvoir, Simone, 3, 105

Debus, Allen, 43, 55
della Porta, Giambattista, 49
Descartes, René, 46
Dinnerstein, Dorothy, 72, 93, 111
Diotima, 24, 29
Dobbs, Betty Jo, 55
Dover, Kenneth, 24–25

Easlea, Brian, 46, 51–52, 60, 64
Ehrenreich, Barbara, 123
Einstein, Albert, 10, 72, 77
Elias, Norbert, 69
Ellman, Mary, 10
Emerson, R. A., 158–59
Erikson, Erik, 108, 172, 175

Fairbairn, W. R. D., 101
Farrington, Benjamin, 36–39, 48
Finkelstein, David, 145
Flax, Jane, 72, 107
Freud, Sigmund, 41, 80, 86, 96,
  101, 109, 113, 118–19

Galen, 39, 44
Gassendi, Pierre, 46
Gay, Peter, 63
Gilligan, Carol, 72, 73, 101
Glanvill, Joseph, 52, 54, 56–60
Golden, Mark, 27
Gomperz, Theodor, 21
Goodfield, June, 115, 125
Greenson, Ralph, 88
Grontkowski, Christine, 23
Guntrip, Harry, 101